THE QUESTING MIND
IS A SALIENT CHARACTERISTIC
OF A FREEMASON

VOLUME I
A COLLECTION OF WRITINGS
BY JOHN L. COOPER III

COLLECTED AND EDITED
BY ALLAN L. CASALOU

THE QUESTING MIND IS A SALIENT
CHARACTERISTIC OF A FREEMASON
VOLUME I
A COLLECTION OF WRITINGS BY JOHN L. COOPER III
Grand Lodge Free and Accepted Masons of California
September 2014, 2015

Book design & editing by Allan L. Casalou
Cover design by Chen Design Associates

Library of Congress Control Number: 2014950319

Printed in the United States of America
by Macoy Publishing and Masonic Supply Co., Inc.
www.macoy.com

*For John and Heather Cooper and for their
children and grandchildren*

CONTENTS

The Point (Spring 1999)   1

The Line (Summer 1999)   3

The Superfice (Fall 1999)   5

From a Superfice to Solid (Winter 1999)   7

The Trouble with History – The Recognition of Prince Hall Freemasonry (Spring 2000)   9

The Two Parallel Lines (Fall 2000)   13

The Wardens' Columns (Winter 2001)   15

The Book of Constitutions (Spring 2001)   17

It's a Secret! (Summer 2001)   19

That Standard or Boundary of Right (Summer 2002)   21

The Compass and the Constitution (Fall 2002)   23

Dialogue Between Ernst and Falk - Lessing addresses Masonic relief in the 18th century (Winter 2002)   25

Recommending a Man to Become a Mason – The key word is fidelity (Spring 2003)   27

The Master and the Lodge – A model of Masonic leadership (Summer 2003)   29

Masonic Colleges (Fall 2003)   31

St. Lawrence and the Treasures (Winter 2003)   33

Moral Architecture (Spring 2004)   35

Freemasonry and the Initiatic Process (Summer 2004)   39

Manifest Destiny and Freemasonry (Fall 2004)   43

Anti-Masonry through the Centuries (Winter 2004)   45

The Royal Art (Spring 2005)   47

The Three Steps Usually Delineated upon the Master's Carpet
(Summer 2005)   49

Freemasonry in the Victorian Era: An Overview (Fall 2005)   51

Interior Illumination and Exterior Brightness (Winter 2006)   53

Let Harmony Prevail (Spring 2006)   55

A Progressive Moral Science Divided Into Different Degrees
(Summer 2006)   57

A Member of It (Fall 2006)   61

The Fraternity and the Flag (Winter 2007)   63

The Home of the Muses (Spring 2007)   67

The Springs Gush Forth (Summer 2007)   69

Who Was Hiram Abiff? (Fall 2007)   71

Beginning the Masonic Journey – The Entered Apprentice
Mason (Winter 2008)   73

Sir Alexander Fleming – Scientist and Freemason (Spring 2008)
His passion for relieving distress led to a moldy discovery   75

Exploring Important Issues in Freemasonry Today - The California
Masonic Symposium (Summer 2008)   77

The Home of the First Grand Lodge (Fall 2008)   79

It's Really About Brotherhood (Oct/Nov 2008)   81

The Lodge at Refreshment (Dec/Jan 2009)   83

No More Than He Really May Deserve – Helping our youth
orders the right way (Feb/Mar 2009)   85

The Beehive and Community Service (Apr/May 2009)   87

The Three Sources of Our Country's Greatness (Jun/Jul 2009)   89

Past Perfect (Aug/Sep 2009)   91

Why Blue? (Oct/Nov 2009)   93

The Templar Connection – The hoax behind one of Masonry's
most popular myths (Dec/Jan 2010)   95

Of the Civil Magistrate, Supreme and Subordinate (Feb/Mar 2010)   99

Choices – Freemasonry is all about choices (Apr/May 2010)   103

A Progressive Moral Science (Jun/Jul 2010)   105

Consider Frederick – From a despotic family and war-torn
country, a Masonic king emerged (Aug/Sep 2010)   107

Back to the Future – How would Masonry look today if history
were rewritten? (Oct/Nov 2010)   109

From a Badge to a Symbol – Emblems to allegories, Masonic
symbols contain different levels of meaning (Dec/Jan 2011)   111

The Indissoluble Chain – To relieve the distressed is a duty
incumbent on all men, but particularly Masons ... (Feb/Mar 2011)   115

The Citadel of Our Safety – Public education's power to unite
(Apr/May 2011)   117

Inquiring Minds Want to Know – The 39 exposés – and
counting – that shape Masonry (Jun/Jul 2011)   121

Death of a Craftsman – The legend and lessons behind a famous
work of craftsmanship (Aug/Sep 2011)   125

The Masonic Explorer – Whither are you traveling?
(Oct/Nov 2011)   129

How Does Your Garden Grow? In Freemasonry, we find the
beauty of life itself (Dec/Jan 2012)   131

Novus Ordo Seclorum – Masonic principles pointed the way
for a new republic (Feb/Mar 2012)   133

A Novel Idea – American Masonry establishes Masonic
youth orders (Apr/May 2012)   137

Masonic Parades as Street Theater – A Mason's behavior in
the 'theater' of life is ever important (Jun/July 2012)   141

Concerning God and Religion (Aug/Sept 2012)   143

One Lodge or Fifty? George Washington and the "American
Doctrine" (Oct/Nov 2012)   147

The Power of the Pen – Gotthold Lessing and Masonic tolerance
(Dec/Jan 2013)   149

The Eighteenth Century Internet – the first flurries of information
exchange took a tangible format (Feb/Mar 2013)   151

Masonic Charity – A Historical Perspective – the fraternal
commitment to relief has defined the institution of Freemasonry
(Apr/May 2013)   155

Look Around – Sir Christopher Wren and the architectural
renaissance in London after the Great Fire (Jun/Jul 2013)   157

Schools of Virtue – Early American lodges provided unprecedented opportunities for young men to learn values and practice
leadership (Aug/Sep 2013)   159

Our Ancient Friend and Brother – The teachings of Pythagoras
continue to inspire our fraternity (Oct/Nov 2013)   163

The Art of Memory (Dec/Jan 2014)   167

A Candid Disquisition – Wellins Calcott and the Masonic culture
of fellowship (Feb/Mar 2014)   169

At a Perpetual Distance (Apr/May 2014)   171

My Brother's Keeper (Jun/Jul 2014)   173

When the Masonic Lodge Was a University – Lodge rooms reflect
our Masonic quest for knowledge (Aug/Sep 2014)   175

FOREWORD

Teaching is all about learning. The best teachers are the best students. This collection of writings is by one of the most interesting students on the subject of Freemasonry.

John Lilburn Cooper III was raised a Master Mason in Anaheim Masonic Lodge No. 207 fifty years ago on September 10, 1964. To commemorate his Golden Anniversary as a Master Mason, I have published this collection of his written contributions to the *California Freemason* magazine, the award-winning member publication of the Grand Lodge of Free and Accepted Masons of the State of California.

I've had the honor to serve as editor of the magazine since 2002 and with each issue, we've been privileged to publish an article by John. He started writing a regular column in 1999 titled *The Winding Staircase.* Volume I of this collection begins with the first publication of that column and ends with his latest article published in August 2014. There are 71 articles in all, which range in subject matter from the meaning of Masonic symbols to historic Masonic events to the ideas of those now famous in Masonic history and lore. Many of the articles give us a look back in time to periods of significance in the craft. They also speak to the modern Mason (or interested person) who is searching for truth and knowledge in his own life. Through these articles, John shares important ideas that are the basis for what he calls "Masonic formation"—the life-long process of becoming a Mason, understanding Masonic teachings and applying them in our daily lives.

Before being elected the 10th grand secretary of the Grand Lodge of California in 1991, John was a leader in public education—first as a high school teacher, then as an administrator, and finally as the superintendent of the Escondido Union High School District in San Diego County. John loves to teach—I think because he loves to learn. He has an insatiable appetite for knowledge—or truth—and he eagerly shares what he learns. He is among the most well-read people I know, but what is most unique about John is his ability to share his knowledge in a way that is approachable by anyone regardless of one's experience or education. John knows that everyone is capable of learning and he has a way of making it so interesting that many of us are more motivated to learn and share than we might have been without knowing him.

John has made many contributions to Freemasonry over the last half century—too numerous to detail in this foreword. Some, however, are directly related to the work in this collection and deserve our attention.

After 35 years of reading and writing about Freemasonry, John helped establish the Institute for Masonic Studies (IMS) sponsored by the Grand Lodge of California. While he may not claim the credit and others have certainly made important contributions of their own, John was and continues to be the driving force behind the IMS. He has never chaired the Institute, but he has seen to its success and continuation. Through the IMS, John has helped inspire a new generation of Masons to study and enjoy the rich history, traditions, symbolism, and philosophy of Freemasonry. He organized the first Masonic symposium in California in 2001. Today, hundreds of Masons and their guests still gather for the symposium annually to explore some interesting aspect of Freemasonry. John also organized the first Masonic colloquium in California in 2013. In addition to the in-person audience, the colloquium is streamed over the Internet to audiences in other parts of the world. Because of its popularity, the next colloquium is scheduled in November 2014 and I won't be surprised if it becomes another annual Masonic education event.

I also won't be surprised if someday it's forgotten that a Mason named John Cooper established these events. His name is not that closely linked to them. But his contributions to the *California Freemason* will endure for centuries. The works contained in this collection will be read for generations. And while some readers might never have had the same privilege I have had to know John personally, they will be inspired by his ideas, his intellect, his humor and his broad view of the world. This is the aim of this book - to widely share the ideas of this extraordinary man and Mason.

John was my predecessor as grand secretary. He served for 17 years and retired in 2008. In 2013, he became the first past grand secretary to be elected grand master of our Grand Lodge. He leaves this office later this year. He will have a lot to reflect upon and be proud of as he enjoys what leadership guru Walter Wright calls the "third third of life."

I imagine John's writing will only increase and evolve over the next few decades.

That's why this collection is titled *Volume I.*

Allan L. Casalou
San Francisco, CA
September 10, 2014

ACKNOWLEDGEMENTS

Publishing a collection of writings is not an endeavor one can do alone. Many hands were involved in this good work.

Of course, all of the heavy lifting was done by John Cooper, himself, who authored each of these articles over the last fifteen years. Magazine publishing is all about deadlines—and getting writers to submit their work on time is sometimes a challenge. Not with John—he writes them overnight, it seems. It's like the thoughts stream from his mind right onto the document in perfect form. It's almost embarrassing to claim that I edit his articles - his work requires very little editing, if any.

The publication of this collection was made possible by my amazing assistant, Lisa Urrizalqui, who never hesitates to take on a new project. When I told her we were going to publish a book—something neither of us had ever done—she said, "Sure!" She had a plan by the end of the day. And she executed it with the skill and efficiency that has become the signature of all her work. We were assisted by the talented communications team at the Grand Lodge—Emily Limón, Sarah Gilbert, and Patrick Clos. I'm so proud of the work they do and I'm honored that they were a part of this project. The cover design is by Chen Design Associates in San Francisco - our design partner for the *California Freemason*. Marilyn Wordlow graciously offered to perform the final copy edit and this is a much better book because of her sharp eye, solid skills, and genuine desire to help.

I want to take this opportunity to thank those who have been a part of our *California Freemason* publishing team over the years. Many people have made contributions of writing, art, photography, and design, so I cannot recognize them all here, but I must name a few. In addition to the communications team mentioned above, the following people have been instrumental in publishing the magazine since 2002: Terry Mendez, Kimberly Rogers-Murawski, Angel Alvarez-Mapp, Laura Normand, Megan Brown, and Michelle Simone. I want to thank the following Grand Masters of the Grand Lodge of California who have appointed me editor over the years: C. Ray Whitaker, M. William Holsinger, Howard D. Kirkpatrick, David R. Doan, Frederick L. Sorsabal, Melvyn B. Stein, Richard Wakefield Hopper, Larry L. Adamson, Kenneth G. Nagel, William J. Bray III, Frank Loui, John F. Lowe, and last, but not least - John L. Cooper III.

There have only been three editors of the *California Freemason* since it was first published in 1954. I want to pay tribute to my two, late predecessors - Newcomb Condee (1898-1974) who was editor from 1954-1974 and Ralph H. Head (1913-2002), editor from 1974-2002. They left behind big shoes to fill and it's an honor to follow them.

THE QUESTING MIND IS A SALIENT CHARACTERISTIC OF A FREEMASON

VOLUME I
A COLLECTION OF WRITINGS
BY JOHN L. COOPER III

THE POINT

By John L. Cooper III
California Freemason, Spring 1999

Many of our Masonic ideas can be traced back to the ancient Greek philosopher Pythagoras, who founded a school teaching a "progressive moral science," much like our own.   By studying the ideas of the Pythagoreans, we may come to a better appreciation of Freemasonry.

The Pythagoreans were the first to elevate mathematics from purely utilitarian aims to a study worth pursuing for its own sake. Their method was different from that of modern science. They were more concerned with the investigation of principles than with the investigation of things. And unlike our science today, which uses general theories and applies them to specific cases, the Pythagoreans began with a specific phenomenon and attempted to use it to discover universal principles. For the Pythagoreans, the study of geometry was not so much a separate mathematical discipline, as it was an investigation of the laws which govern the universe itself. And so it is for us as Freemasons.

The heart of their philosophy was the concept of number, which was described as "the principle, the source and the root of all things." And at the very center of this philosophy was the concept of monad or unity: the point.

Unity is the principle of all things and the most dominant of all that is. All things emanate from it and it emanates from nothing. It is indivisible and it is everything in power. It is immutable and never departs from its own nature through multiplication ($1 \times 1 = 1$). Everything that is intelligible and not yet created exists in it; the nature of ideas. God himself, the soul, the beautiful and the good, and every intelligible essence, such as beauty itself, equality itself, for we conceive each of these things as being one and as existing in itself.

The point brings to mind the ideas of initiation and beginning. It also suggests initiative, inception, genesis, originality, unity, singleness, isolation, concentration, self-consciousness and so forth.

As Masons, we are quite familiar with the symbol of the point within the circle. This marvelous device graphically represents the relationship between the individual and the Great Architect of the Universe. It is formed by first placing the point of a compass upon a piece of paper and then circumscribing a circle around that central point. It will be observed that each point of the circle thus traced is equidistant from the central point. Hence, the Great Architect of the Universe, whom we all adore, is omnipresent in our lives.

Further, the circle represents the boundary line beyond which we should not allow our passions to lead us, lest we lose that unity and common purpose that is so central to our Craft.

The point within the circle is also the alchemical symbol of the sun. That sun is the indwelling spirit within each of us and represents that part of us which our ritual states will "never, never, die." The sun is the center of our solar system, about which revolve all the planets and (apparently) the signs of the zodiac. It is the source of light and life and was therefore regarded as a symbol of God by the ancients. Even today in modern Freemasonry it is an emblem of the Most High.

This is an important clue to the inner significance of the Master Mason degree, as well. For that degree, when rightly understood, provides a complete summary of the entire chemical work. This is not the place to enter into an in-depth discussion of that work, but the inquisitive Mason is encouraged to search out this meaning on his own.

There is clearly a great deal of meaning which can be found in even the most simple symbol. We have provided a few clues, but is up to you to follow them to their logical conclusion. In our next installment, we shall investigate the nature of duality, represented by a line.

THE LINE

By John L. Cooper III
California Freemason, Summer 1999

In our first installment, we examined the nature of unity represented by the point. From the point proceeds the line, representing duality or the number 2. The number 2 signifies duplication, repetition, wisdom and science, opposition, polarity, antitheses, succession, sequence, continuation, diffusion, separation, radiation, subordinate, dependence, and subconsciousness. The reader would do well to look up each of these words in a dictionary, as doing so will provide many insights into the nature of duality.

The most obvious representation of the number 2 within a Masonic lodge are the two brazen pillars in the northwest corner of the lodge room. These pillars are surmounted by globes, a terrestrial globe in the north and a celestial globe in the south. While nothing is mentioned about any such globes in the Old Testament description of King Solomon's Temple, they are important symbolically. The celestial globe represents the essential forces of nature, the divine origin of creation and the principles by which the universe is governed. Thus, it symbolizes the underlying unity of all.

By contrast, the terrestrial globe represents manifestation, the physical world and the multiplicity of things. The material world proceeds from the divine, just as the line proceeds from the point. The point is finite and limited, but a line contains an infinite number of points within it. The line is therefore unlimited.

The Pythagoreans, an ancient Greek school much like our own fraternity and the source of much of our Masonic philosophy, described this idea in terms of matter (the indefinite) and form (limit). These were "the two most essential elements which are absolutely necessary for the manifestation of phenomenal reality."

If one represents the principle of unity from which all things arise, then 2, the dyad, represents duality, the beginning of multiplicity, the beginning of strife, yet also the possibility of logos, the relation of one thing to another.

In Greek philosophy, the "logos" was the means by which Creation of the world took place, the "Expression" or "Word" of the Creator. Although Christianity took this phrase over and applied it to Jesus Christ, its use is older and more universal. In Greek philosophy the "logos" was not only the "act of Creation" itself, but also the means by which Creation took place. In other words, the "Word," or "Expression of God," was responsible for Creation, and was identified with God himself.

An astute reader will not overlook the significance of the Word in our own Masonic allegory. In this sense, it represents knowledge of the divine. When the Master's "Word" is lost, what is alluded to is the loss of our intimate connection with the Great Architect. The Master Mason is encouraged in our rituals to go in search of that which was lost, to reestablish a conscious connection with the Supreme Being.

The two pillars also establish a line between the outside world and the sacred space inside a lodge room for the first time, is placed between the pillars to reinforce the distinction between these two worlds. And every time we step from the outside world into our lodge, we should also be reminded of the importance of leaving behind the mundane affairs of the outer world.

Another important idea conveyed by the principle of duality is that of opposites: light and darkness, black and white, good and evil, male and female, order and chaos. Within a lodge room are many examples of the principle of opposites. The black and white tessellated floor, the sun and the moon, east and west are just some examples.

What is important for us to understand is that these symbols are meant to convey that opposites exist within each of us. Each of us has within himself aspects of good and aspects of evil. Our task is to understand and eventually reconcile these opposite forces within ourselves. For in truth, these apparent opposites are actually just different qualities of the same thing. Good and evil are really just aspects of the quality of goodness. Darkness is naught but the absence of light. We will discuss this idea further in our examination of the superfice or the number 3.

THE SUPERFICE

By John L. Cooper III
California Freemason, Fall 1999

In the first two installments, we looked at two of the symbols used in the Fellow Craft degree from the science of geometry, namely "The Point", and "The Line". In the first article we explored one meaning of "The Point", which was unity, and the roots of our understanding of this concept from the philosopher Pythagoras was discussed. In "The Line" the concept of duality or of "opposing forces" was discussed. In both, the Freemason was encouraged to look beyond the obvious symbol, and to apply these meanings within his own life. The same may be said for our discussion of the third concept, "The Superfice".

A superfice is a flat plane in geometry. A point has no length or breadth; a line has length and breadth. If two lines cross each other they create a superfice because together they establish length in two directions. A line may be said to be a symbol of infinity, for it extends infinitely in two directions, and (in Euclidean geometry) the ends never meet. It is only when we arrive at the concept of a superfice that we enter what might be said to be the human dimension. A superfice creates a surface, or more poetically, a stage, upon which human action can take place. There are several possible Masonic interpretations of this stage, but one that is obvious to all who have read the longer form of the first degree lecture in our *Monitor*, is the lodge itself. The lecture puts it thus:

> The form of a lodge is oblong. It extends from east to west and from north to south, and it is said to be thus extensive to denote the universality of Masonry and to teach us that a Mason's charity should be equally extensive; for in every country and in every clime are Masons to be found.

A Fellow Craft Mason who is properly instructed in one Masonic meaning of "The Superfice" should be caused to reflect on what he heard (or read) as an Entered Apprentice Mason about the form of the lodge. The Fellow Craft earns his wages within the lodge, and in doing so, he must become aware of the two dimensions which constitute it, and which are referenced in the Entered Apprentice lecture. The first of these Masonic dimensions is universality. Freemasonry embraces men of "every country, sect and opinion," and is "one sacred band or society of friends and brothers, among whom no contention should ever exist, but that noble contention, or rather emulation, of who best can work and best agree." The first and primary dimension of a Masonic lodge is that it is universal, and this universality, like one line of the superfice, has no end or boundary. There are no exclusions in Freemasonry because of religion, race, or color.

The second principle, the second dimension making up the "oblong form" of the lodge, is charity, or love. If Freemasonry embraces men of all faiths and all social classes, of all races and all nationalities, then there are no limits on the exercise of brotherly love. My obligation to love others as a Freemason extends equally to all, and is without limit. The Fellow Craft is later told that, "Geometry [is] the first and noblest of sciences, and the basis upon which the superstructure of Freemasonry is erected." Indeed it is. The geometric form of the superfice is a symbol of the lodge, where Masonic work begins. And undergirding our work as Masons must be an understanding that the superfice, as a part of geometry, is the plane upon which we carry out our Masonic work. That plane, symbolized by the lodge itself, reminds us that our charity – our love for the brethren – must be equally extensive. And we are further encouraged that we will find co-workers to help us with the Great Work wherever Freemasonry is established, "for in every country and in every clime are Masons to be found."

FROM A SUPERFICE TO A SOLID

By John L. Cooper III
California Freemason, Winter 1999

This is the fourth in a series of discussions on the meaning of geometry, and especially as it is explained in the lecture of the Fellow Craft degree. As we have seen in the three articles before, the candidate is taught that Freemasonry and geometry are intertwined, and that a proper understanding of geometry is an important means of understanding Freemasonry. Why is this so? And what can we learn from a study of the principles of geometry that can inform our daily life?

The lectures of the Fellow Craft degree are not really a short course in geometry. On the surface they seem to imply that a well-educated Fellow Craft ought to know something about the seven liberal arts and sciences, and ought to know more about geometry than about any of the seven. Some writers have assumed that William Preston, who wrote our lectures, was trying to provide a course in education at a time when widespread public education was rare. If so, he went about it in a strange manner, for the lectures do no more than touch upon the subject of science in general, and of geometry in particular. Moreover, Preston did not invent the subject matter of his lectures. He merely arranged material in use in the lodges in the eighteenth century. The association of geometry with Freemasonry goes back to the *Old Charges* which pre-date the grand lodge era. A manuscript of 1583 stated that geometry "...teacheth a man the met and measure of earth and all other things." (Grand Lodge Ms., and edition of the *Old Charges*)

Geometry is thus said to be of primary importance to Freemasonry long before William Preston wrote his *Illustrations of Masonry* in 1772, the source of our current lectures. And if it teaches a man the "measure of ... all other things," then it has to do more with what man is than what he has learned.

It has to do with the heart, and not with the intellect. This interpretation fits nicely with the explanation of geometry as having to do with a point, a line, a superfice, and a solid. For as a solid has length, breadth, and thickness, so man, if he is to be whole, must be considered as a totality.

Contemporary psychology has taught us to understand the dysfunctional personality, and this is frequently defined to mean a personality that stresses some character trait at the expense of another. A dysfunctional personality is not whole. And for Freemasonry itself to be whole it has to develop a man's mind while developing his spirit. A whole Mason is one who recognizes that God is the source of life, and shapes his life in accordance with his understanding of the God that he worships. A whole Mason is both inwardly directed, and outwardly directed. He respects himself as a creature of his Creator, and respects the society in which he lives as an outward extension of the wholeness of his inner life.

A Fellow Craft Mason who understands the importance of geometry will use the tools of a Fellow Craft Mason to shape his life, in accordance with its principles. And in doing so, will illustrate the meaning of a solid in geometry: From a point to a line, from a line to a superfice, and from a superfice to a solid. "Solidity", which we translate as "wholeness", has been attained.

THE TROUBLE WITH HISTORY
The Recognition of Prince Hall Freemasonry

By John L. Cooper III
California Freemason, Spring 2000

This issue of the *California Freemason* magazine is devoted to a celebration of the 150th Anniversary of the founding of the Masonic Grand Lodge of California.

You will read articles elsewhere telling about the founding of Grand Lodge, and some of the events celebrating the 150th anniversary. *The Winding Staircase*, the quarterly publication of the Institute for Masonic Studies, is a place for reflection upon some of the larger questions in our Masonic life, and in this article I invite you to reflect upon the idea of history.

What is history anyway? How do we know that what we think of as history of Freemasonry in California is accurate? Is it possible that history is shaped by those who wrote it? Is history shaped by the times in which it is written?

I invite you to reflect with me on this subject as it pertains to a complete change in our understanding of that subject of exclusive territorial jurisdiction, and the recognition of the Prince Hall Grand Lodge of California and Hawaii in 1995.

In 1995 the Grand Lodge of California voted at its annual communication to recognize the Prince Hall Grand Lodge of California and Hawaii, effective February 1, 1996. The vote was overwhelming—92% of those casting ballots favored such recognition. It was obvious to those who saw the results that the delegates to Grand Lodge had spoken decisively. From that point forward there would be two equal Masonic grand lodges in California, sharing the same territory, and mutually co-existing. This historic vote (following a similar action by the Prince Hall Grand Lodge the previous July) seemed to rectify an ancient wrong, and to usher in a new era of pride that the perceived racism of not recognizing the Prince Hall Grand Lodge was now a thing of the past.

The effective date of the mutual recognition occurred just a few days before the death of Past Grand Master Edward H. Siems, our then senior past grand master and past grand secretary. A towering Mason of his generation, Brother Ed had almost single-handedly led Grand Lodge to build the California Masonic Memorial Temple atop Nob Hill in San Francisco in the 1950s while grand treasurer, and went on to become one of the most highly respected grand secretaries in the country through his seventeen years of service to our grand lodge. In 1977, he served as president of the Conference of Grand Secretaries of North America, an honor afforded only a few grand secretaries in any generation. And it was as Grand Master in 1949 that he led the Conference of Grand Masters of Masons in North America to decisively oppose the 1947 action of the Grand Lodge of Massachusetts in recognizing Prince Hall Freemasonry as legitimate. Those who knew did not fail to note the irony that the Grand Lodge of California recognized Prince Hall Freemasonry as legitimate for the first time in its history just three days before the death of this monumental California Freemason who had led American grand lodges to reject Prince Hall Freemasonry two generations before.

In 1949, when Edward H. Siems was grand master of Masons in California, the United States was a very different place than it was in 1996. Racial segregation was the law of the land in roughly half the American states, and although another past grand master, Harry S. Truman, had abolished racial segregation in the American Armed Forces after the Second World War, American society was still largely segregated along racial lines. Freemasonry was segregated as well, although the *California Masonic Code*, then as now, forbade the exclusion of an applicant on the basis of race. The issue for Grand Master Siems in 1949, however, was not race. It was the issue of exclusive territorial jurisdiction. The doctrine then prevailing was that there could be one, and only one, Masonic grand lodge in any American state. The recognition of Prince Hall Freemasonry by the Grand Lodge of Massachusetts upset this venerable tradition, and threatened the doctrine of exclusive territorial jurisdiction. The Grand Lodge of California led the charge against this breach of the citadel, and in 1949 the Grand Lodge of Massachusetts backed down. The doctrine of exclusive territorial jurisdiction was saved.

Edward H. Siems was not a racist. His position was as logical in 1949 as the position of the Grand Lodge of California was in 1995 when we discarded our previous position. What had changed was our perception of history. In 1949, the issue of exclusive territorial jurisdiction seemed to be an immutable landmark of Freemasonry. In 1995, our concept of what was immutable had changed.

Therefore, the question before us is, is history only relative? Is truth defined by the social context? Is truth defined by the time in which we live? Is there any such thing as absolute truth? For Freemasons this is not an idle question. Brotherly love, relief and truth are the three principal tenets of Freemasonry. But what is truth? If truth is one thing in 1949, and another in 1995, is there any such thing as truth? If all truth is relative, then how is my truth any better than your truth?

The answer, in part, is explained by the philosophy of history we hold. If history is seen as the story of a particular time or period, then we must be clear as to whether we are telling the whole story, or only a part of it.

Most contemporary accounts of the Prince Hall controversy of 1947 to 1949 only tell the story from the point of view of the "regular" grand lodges. Few, if any, told the story broadly enough to include the impact of these events on the Prince Hall grand lodges of the day. Would we retell the story if we wrote it today? Would our account talk about the impact of the de-recognition of Prince Hall Freemasonry by the Grand Lodge of Massachusetts on the Prince Hall Grand Lodge of Massachusetts? Would it talk about the impact on the Prince Hall Grand Lodge of California?

These questions are raised by way of illustration, and to point out that what we consider as history may only be part of the story. What we consider to be history in the year 2000 may turn out to be only part of the story for a generation to come. As you read the history of Freemasonry in California in this magazine, consider, if you will, what part of the story we are leaving out. Consider, if you will, what a future generation will think of our telling of the story of our history today. Is it possible that the answer to the question, "What is truth?" lies in the Masonic understanding that truth is always an ideal? A quest? If truth is not relative, and yet not absolute, is it instead a "work in progress"? If so, then Freemasonry provides an important answer to our basic question. Truth will change because truth is actually a process of growth in understanding. As long as we can accept that our truth today may be better understood tomorrow, we can escape from the trap of relativism.

Yes, there is such a thing as truth. No, I don't possess it all today. For tomorrow I may receive "further light in Masonry" that will help me understand today's truth in ways that I could never have imagined!

THE TWO PARALLEL LINES

By John L. Cooper III
California Freemason, Fall 2000

The monitorial lecture of the first degree of Masonry, after explaining that the point within a circle teaches us that we need to keep our passions under control so as not to harm others, goes on to say:

> This circle is supported by two perpendicular parallel lines, representing Saint John the Baptist and Saint John the Evangelist, and on its top rest the Holy Writings. In tracing its circumference we necessarily touch upon the parallel lines and also upon the Holy Bible; and while a Mason keeps himself thus circumscribed, it is impossible that he can materially err.

Why would a Mason "materially err" if he ignored the meaning of this symbol in his life? And what are two Christian saints doing in a ritual that is for Masons of all religious faiths, and not for Christians alone? What is the meaning of this symbol for our Jewish brethren? Are they expected to understand this reference from a religious point of view?

Or is this symbol the remains of our medieval heritage, a time when all members of the Craft were Catholic Christians? Is there anything about these two Christian saints that has universal meaning regardless of a Mason's individual religious faith?

Some scholars believe that these two saints were chosen not for what they taught, but rather for the symbolism associated with the location of their saint's day in the Christian calendar. The Feast Day of St. John the Baptist is June 24, and the Feast Day of St. John the Evangelist is December 27. Those days are close to the summer solstice (June 21) and the winter solstice (December 21). However that may be, there is no observation about that in our ritual. The ritual merely states that the two parallel lines represent these two saints, and that they are associated in some fashion with the Holy Bible resting on the top of the two parallel lines. While it is possible that these two saints came into Freemasonry as the result of their association with the summer and winter solstices, there is no inference in this lecture to lead us to make that assumption. Is there an easier explanation? I think that there is.

In the Christian scriptures, St. John the Baptist was portrayed as an ascetic, a hermit who lived in the desert near the River Jordan. "Now John wore clothing of camel's hair with a leather belt around his waist, and his food was locusts and wild honey." (Matthew 3:4, NSRV) John the Baptist is a proclaimer of the judgment of God against sin and evil. His message was, "Repent, for the kingdom of heaven has come near." (Verse 2) In this context, the word "repent" means to "turn around" or to "go back". The message of John the Baptist is that we are accountable to God for our actions, and we ignore this accountability at our own peril.

St. John the Evangelist, on the other hand, is portrayed as the Apostle of Love. To him is attributed the First Epistle of John, and that epistle has much to say about brotherly love.

> He that saith he is in the light, and hateth his brother, is in darkness even until now. He that loveth his brother abideth in the light, and there is none occasion of stumbling in him. (I John 2:10-11, AV)

In each of the three degrees of Masonry we were asked what we most desired, and the response is universally, "Light!" St. John the Evangelist teaches us that brotherly love must accompany this search for light, or we sorely deceive ourselves about the results. The search for light in Freemasonry is a symbol of the search for truth. But unless that search for truth is within the context of brotherly love, the light may turn out to be darkness in the end.

The ritual teaches us that a Mason will not make a mistake if he understands the symbol of the two parallel lines representing St. John the Baptist and St. John the Evangelist. In universal Masonic terms, it might be said that a Mason must temper his search for truth by keeping in mind two things. The first is that truth must stand the test of God's judgment. The second is that truth must be pursued within the context of love for others. Neither by itself is sufficient for a Mason. Our pursuit of the truth must encompass a passion for justice and a love for our fellow human beings. One without the other leads to a distortion in our lives. Freemasons should not tolerate religious bigotry nor racial and ethnic hatred, but neither should they so pursue justice that they forget to love. St. John the Baptist and St. John the Evangelist are symbols of a commitment to justice and right on the one hand, and to love of others in meeting that commitment on the other hand.

Love that does not recognize the need for justice becomes unjust, and justice that does not recognize the need for love becomes cruel and inhuman. These two symbols meet in God, represented by the Holy Bible on the top. Yet it is only by our understanding of His concepts of both justice and love that we keep our own concepts in balance. And thus "while a Mason keeps himself thus circumscribed, it is impossible that he can materially err."

The Wardens' Columns

By John L. Cooper III
California Freemason, Winter 2001

There are two peculiar pieces of equipment in a Masonic lodge that have no explanation in our ritual. Masonic scholars have reached no conclusions as to the origin, function or purpose of the wardens' columns.

In California lodges these are foot tall wooden imitations of Ionic columns. They have a particular use in showing when the lodge is at labor and when it is at refreshment; the position of the columns being reversed when the lodge changes from one activity to another.

But there is no explanation in the ritual as to why these two pieces of equipment show that, nor is that an explanation of why they have the form that they do. However, we can guess an origin by knowing something about how early degrees were conferred, and I suggest that their origin is to be found by taking a look at how lodges customarily functioned two centuries ago.

Lodges in the eighteenth century usually met in taverns; in a room that provided sufficient privacy to conduct Masonic ceremonies. These rooms were usually furnished with tables, and when a candidate was to receive a degree, the tables would be taken down and placed against the wall so that there would be room to do the degree work.

At meetings when no degrees work was to be performed the tables remained in place. The tables were placed together in the center of the room so that the officers could sit around the table, talking to their neighbors and enjoying the conviviality that such lodge meetings afforded. We do not eat nor drink in our lodge rooms today, but two centuries ago they did. If you visit the museum at the Grand Temple in London, the home of the United Grand Lodge of England, you will see magnificent Masonic tableware, including beautiful rum punchbowls with Masonic symbols on the outside. These punchbowls were conveniently placed around the table so that the officers and brethren could help themselves during the dinner and festivities, which followed; and from other sources we know that our ancient brethren managed to enjoy themselves even to excess on more than one occasion!

The entertainment, if it can be called that, was usually the rehearsing of Masonic lectures by well skilled brethren who had memorized the old question and answer lectures. I imagine that if mistakes were made in the recitation of those old lectures, the past masters of those days were as unforgiving in their comments as past masters are wont to be today!

It was the custom also to smoke in lodge in those days. The "devil weed" had come to England with Sir Walter Raleigh in the time of Queen Elizabeth, and by the eighteenth century, pipe smoking was a popular habit. However, it was considered to be distracting to the rehearsal of the lectures to be reaching for more rum punch, or filling one's pipe, when the lectures were in progress. The master therefore called the lodge from labor to refreshment with some frequency so that the brethren could enjoy their pipes and their rum punch. After an appropriate break in the proceedings the master would call his lodge from refreshment to labor again, usually with the sound of the gavel in the East, of course, because that was the side of the table on which he was seated. The brethren would instantly stop their conversation, put down their glasses of punch, and lay their pipes aside, for the "sound of the gavel in the East" was their cue that it was time to pay attention to the lectures which constituted the teaching of Freemasonry.

In order to remind the brethren that they were now at labor, the Masonic term they used for returning to the serious part of the evening, the wardens would use their columns. If the senior warden stood his column upright in front of him on the table, it was a sign that the lodge was at labor, and everyone should pay attention and stop talking. When the junior warden had his column upright, the lodge was at refreshment, and the brethren could disport themselves in the usual manner, as long as they did not violate any of the obligations of a brother toward another brother. If anything, our ancient brethren were courteous to a fault, and whether at labor or refreshment, never engaged in behavior which would have embarrassed the lodge nor caused "injury to a brother in his person or good name."

We have inherited this ancient tradition, and still call from labor to refreshment and from refreshment to labor. Today this is usually associated with the conferral of a part of our degree work, but its use is not limited to that function. Properly speaking, the master of a lodge may call his brethren from labor to refreshment when it is desirable to do so. The columns remind us that some Masonic work is serious, and requires our full attention; and some Masonic work is less serious, and allows us to have fun and enjoy one another's company. If any lesson is to be learned from the use of the wardens' columns it is that whether at work, or at play, we never cease to be Masons. We are always under an obligation to act decorously and behave in a manner appropriate to a Mason. After all, that's what sets us apart from so much of the rest of society.

THE BOOK OF CONSTITUTIONS

By John L. Cooper III
California Freemason, Spring 2001

In the lecture of the third degree, a mysterious emblem appears called "The Book of Constitutions Guarded by the Tiler's Sword." When the long-form of the lecture is given, the explanation of this emblem is hardly self-explanatory. Here is what is says:

> The Book of Constitutions Guarded by the Tiler's Sword reminds us that we should be ever watchful and guarded in our thoughts, words and actions, particularly when before the enemies of Masonry; ever bearing in remembrance those truly Masonic virtues, silence and circumspection.

That we should be so reminded is well and good, but that hardly explains the emblem. The tiler's sword is simple enough, but what is the Book of Constitutions? And why does it need to be guarded? The Book of Constitutions appears again in the charge to the master of the lodge in the Installation Ceremony. The master is shown the Book of Constitutions, and told that "...you are expected diligently to search [the Book of Constitutions] and from time to time to cause its contents to be read in your lodge, that none may remain ignorant of the precepts it enjoins, or of the ordinances which it promulgates." That admonition is not much more enlightening than the explanation in the lecture of the third degree. Our custom is to hold up a copy of the *California Masonic Code (CMC)* at that point in the Installation Ceremony as representing the Book of Constitutions.

The *CMC* is a book almost 275 pages in length, and its title page says that it contains the "Constitution and Ordinances" of the Grand Lodge. Note the use of the singular "Constitution" rather than "Constitutions" of the lecture, and of the Installation Ceremony. Is the *CMC* really the Book of Constitutions alluded to in our ritual? And if so, why is one singular and one plural? And do we really expect the master of the lodge to read the entire *CMC* to his lodge during the year? Here, indeed, is a mystery, but one which has a rather simple solution.

The earliest Masonic lodges possessed copies of what they called the *Gothic Constitutions*. Unlike modern law codes, such as the *CMC*, the "constitutions" (note the plural) contained the legendary history of the craft. Portions from these constitutions were read to candidates at the making of a Mason, along with other ceremonies with which we would be somewhat familiar today. Indeed lodges felt that these constitutions were so important that if they did not possess a copy they were deemed to be irregular lodges. When the first grand lodge was formed in 1717 in London, England, lodges were still using these old constitutions as a part of their ceremonies. But with the rapid growth of new lodges after the formation of grand lodge in 1717, there were not enough of these old constitutions to go around. In addition, it was increasingly felt that the old constitutions should be modernized to respond to the emerging needs of the new lodges. Accordingly, in 1723 Grand Lodge approved a new Book of Constitutions which were ordered to be used by the lodges in place of the old *Gothic Constitutions*. The title of this 1723 work is *The Constitutions of the Free-Masons, Containing the History, Charges, Regulations, etc., of that most Ancient and Right Worshipful Fraternity*. From that date on Freemasonry had a new Book of Constitutions, and for more than a century it was the only Book of Constitutions authorized for use by lodges at the making of a Mason.

Fully half of this new book contained the legendary history of the craft familiar from the old *Gothic Constitutions*. At a later time this legendary history would be dropped from Masonic instruction to candidates, not only because it was so lengthy, but because Masons gradually felt that the legendary history of the craft was not needed. The developed ritual replaced the reading of the legendary history, and since it was no longer needed, it was dropped. The second half of the *Constitutions of 1723*, which consisted of six articles called "charges", became the nucleus of Masonic law as it developed in the nineteenth century, and which eventually found its way into our present-day *California Masonic Code*.

The *Constitutions of 1723* consisted of a book in two parts, and when the first part was discarded, the second half was called simply "The Constitution", and has remained so to this day.

But ritual is a conservative thing, and the old teachings about the original Book of Constitutions remained a part of it. Although the Book of Constitutions known by our ancient brethren had disappeared, Masons were still told (in the lecture of the third degree) that it was to teach them to "be ever watchful and guarded". And the master of the lodge was still told that he should "cause its contents to be read" in his lodge. The meaning of all this today is symbolic, for although it would be valuable for a lodge to become familiar with some aspects of the *California Masonic Code*, no one expects us to derive moral instruction from it, much less listen to it read in lodge in its entirety. The words of our ritual hearken back to an earlier day in Freemasonry, a simpler time, and are a relic of a by-gone era, which we none-the-less still treasure. Silence and circumspection are still Masonic virtues, even if we no longer have the old Book of Constitutions to remind us of them.

It's a Secret!

By John L. Cooper III
California Freemason, Summer, 2001

Freemasonry is not a secret society. Its meeting places are well known, its members wear rings and pins identifying them as such, and Grand Lodge is committed to a greater visibility of Freemasonry in the eyes of the public through its public relations program. It is a society that has secrets, of course. We meet in tiled sessions behind closed doors to which non-Masons are not admitted; we have modes of recognition whereby we can confirm that a man has been made a Mason; and we print a large part of our ceremonies in code so that those who are unfamiliar with the degrees cannot read the text. Why? If we are not a secret society, why are we concerned about all that?

The *California Masonic Code (CMC)*, the basic law governing Freemasonry in California, makes it clear that revealing these secrets to those not entitled to the same can result the filing of charges of unmasonic conduct, and can even result in expulsion from the fraternity. Section 32020 of the *CMC* makes it very clear that,

> The following breaches of faith ... constitute unmasonic conduct sufficient to support the filing of charges against a Mason: ... Disclosure of secret or confidential matters to a non-Mason, [or] Reducing secret work to writing ... (Writing, in this case, means writing the portions of the ritual which are presently in code out in plain English).

We are thus quite serious about keeping some things secret in an organization that we do not consider to be a secret society.

There have been occasions on which the degrees and ceremonies of some of the concordant and appendant bodies have demonstrated to the public, with permission, of course, and with appropriate modification so that the secret work of those degrees and ceremonies were deleted first. But these precedents do not apply to the Grand Lodge of California or its ritual. The *CMC* is clear that secret work is to remain just that – confined to those entitled to the same as Masons.

In earlier columns of *The Winding Staircase*, we have discussed the various symbols of our degrees, and those symbols have been tangible things – ashlars, the point within a circle, and similar objects which can be seen and touched, as well as explained. Is Masonic secrecy a symbol too?

I suggest that it is, and that to understand its symbolic meaning within Freemasonry is to understand why we cannot and will not give up that which can only be communicated to those entitled to the same.

The right to privacy is an important and fundamental human right. The Constitution of the State of California affirms this right in Article I, the article which is the California equivalent of the Bill of Rights of the United States Constitution. Totalitarian governments do not give their citizens the right to privacy; constitutional governments do. Without the right to privacy, most other rights are in jeopardy. And it is here that Masonic secrecy takes on its symbolic content, because it is a symbol of privacy. Privacy is essential to trust, and trust is essential to brotherhood. Privacy has nothing to do with wrongdoing, and indeed, our Masonic obligations make it clear that the secrets of a Master Mason specifically exclude such acts. These secrets of a Mason have rather to do with extending to a brother Mason the right to privacy which respects his integrity as an individual. We cannot be close to one another, which is what brotherhood implies, without becoming privy to the closely held beliefs and feelings of one another. That we will not disclose them improperly is an obligation of brotherhood, and our promise not to do so is the basis of trust for one another.

Seen in the light, Masonic secrecy, like other symbols of Freemasonry, relates to a deep respect for one another as the foundation of true brotherhood. Privacy is thus every bit as much a tenet of Freemasonry as brotherly love, relief, and truth, because it is essential to the exercise of brotherly love, in the first place. If the symbol disappears from Freemasonry, trust will suffer, and thus brotherhood will diminish. If we maintain Masonic secrecy as properly understood, we promote an atmosphere in which trust and brotherhood will flourish.

That Standard or Boundary of Right

By John L. Cooper III
California Freemason, Summer, 2002

Freemasonry is dedicated to the pursuit of truth, and to a deeper understanding of the symbolism through which truth is often communicated. Some symbols are concrete, and some are abstract. For example, in the first degree of Masonry, the rough and perfect ashlars are concrete emblems of personal development. They are easily explained, and easily understood. Other symbols are more abstract, such as the four cardinal virtues. There are surely more than four virtues that are important to the personal development of a Mason, but these four stand symbolically for all the rest. As abstractions they are more difficult to explain, and may be more difficult to understand. One of these – justice – is particularly challenging, because "justice" can all too easily be used to defend and support a personal prejudice as well as the neutral and impartial application of a uniform standard. It is no accident that "justify" is a verb related to "justice", but with a pejorative connotation.

Freemasonry insists that there is a universal standard against which justice is measured. In the words of the ritual, it is the "standard or boundary of right which enables us to render unto every man his just due, without distinction." The words "without distinction" are critical to an understanding of justice. Without impartiality, justice is its inverse – injustice. Justice should be a Masonic passion as well as a Masonic virtue. It should be a passion that causes us to identify with the victims of injustice, as well as to regulate our own conduct by its principles. Such passion may result in a commitment to the correction of injustice, and a life devoted to the pursuit of justice on behalf of others.

While we tend to think of commitment to the cause of justice as an organized endeavor, it can also be a simple response to injustice, a response that may even be spontaneous. When Rosa Parks, tired at the end of a long day of work, refused to move to the back of the bus to sit in a seat reserved for her race, she sparked the civil rights revolution of the 1950s and 1960s. She was not a part of any organized program to end injustice for her race – she just would not put up any more with the indignity and injustice of racial segregation.

There is another story about justice involving a young German soldier during World War II. His story is not a passionate commitment to a great cause for justice, but rather a simple and spontaneous response to injustice. As with many such simple and spontaneous acts that daily fills our lives, it was his understanding of the real meaning of justice that shaped his response to injustice. The story was given to me by Bro. Mark Sandstrom, past master of Covina Lodge No. 334, and with it I close:

> During the dark days of World War II, amid the horrors that were being perpetrated by the Nazi regime, there were pinpoints of light and nobility. One such source of noble light was a German soldier, Private Joseph Schultz. Sent to Yugoslavia shortly after the invasion, Schultz was a loyal young German soldier, filled with what he had perceived to be an ideal worthy of his dedication. One day, while on duty, the sergeant called out eight names, Schultz's among them. Thinking that they were going out on a routine patrol, the soldiers set out. As they made their way over a hill, they came upon eight Yugoslavians, five men and three women. Only after they had drawn to within 50 feet of them, a distance from which any marksman could shoot the eye out of a pheasant, the soldiers realized what their mission was. The sergeant barked out his orders and the eight soldiers lined up. "Ready!" he shouted and they raised their rifles. "Aim" ... and they focused their sights. Suddenly, in the silence that hung heavy in the air, they heard the thud of a rifle butt hitting the ground and as the sergeant and the seven other soldiers turned to look, they saw Private Schultz walking toward the Yugoslavians. Ignoring an order to come back, Schultz walked the fifty feet to the mound of the hill and joined hands with the five men and three women. After a moment of stunned silence, the sergeant yelled, "Fire!" and Private Schultz died, mingling his blood with those innocent men and women.

Justice is that standard or boundary of right.

The Compass and the Constitution

By John L. Cooper III
California Freemason, Fall 2002

Each September, Masons in California celebrate the U.S. Constitution —that beacon of freedom written in Philadelphia in the summer of 1787. It is the oldest such document in existence, and is not only the symbol of our freedom but also its guarantee. After more than 200 years, it still symbolizes that people can govern themselves.

The new American Republic was an experiment in self-government. Once it gained independence from Great Britain, very few of the established nations of the day expected the American Revolution to result in anything more than the creation of a collection of tyrannical states. But they were wrong. The freedom won in the Revolution endured largely due to the U.S. Constitution and its principle of constitutionalism.

We know that many Masons were involved in writing our Constitution. Not so widely known is that the principle on which the Constitution is based is Masonic – one whose symbol is the compass. Masons such as George Washington (who presided over the Constitutional Convention) and Benjamin Franklin (the oldest delegate) knew and understood the use of the compass as a Masonic symbol. They knew that this symbol could be transformed into an instrument of government that would guarantee the liberties won in the hard-fought battles of the American Revolution.

The compass is an emblem of the *limitation of power*. We are taught to use it to "keep our passions within due bounds towards all mankind." We are to use it to respect the boundary between our own desires and needs and the desires and needs of others. This is the principle of constitutionalism. The noble words with which the Preamble begins, "We the people of the United States," are followed by clause after clause of limitations on how the people are to exercise those rights and powers for good or for ill. Our freedoms have survived because we have accepted the principle that the powers inherent to the people are expected to be limited.

It would be interesting to know if the Masons at the Constitutional Convention explained this to the non-Mason delegates. In all probability, the non-Masons did not know the connection between Masonic teachings and what they were trying to create. But we may be thankful that the Masons understood the use of the compass and that constitutionalism as well as the Constitution became the cornerstone of our nation. Respect for the rule of law and respect for the Constitution are Masonic ideals. It is therefore most fitting that we honor the Constitution of the United States each September and honor constitutionalism every time we place the compass on our altar when a Masonic lodge is at work.

Dialogue Between Ernst and Falk
Lessing addresses Masonic relief in the Eighteenth century

By John L. Cooper III
California Freemason, Winter 2002

Masonic relief for the less fortunate as an organized activity by Freemasons is often thought to be a modern phenomenon. Many people think of Masonic charities such as the Shriners hospitals or the Scottish Rite language centers as a purely modern invention within Freemasonry, something newly created in the twentieth century to meet a perceived need to "reach out" to the non-Masonic world through organized charity. It may come as a surprise to learn that "Masonic outreach" is more than two centuries old, and a commentary on its function within Freemasonry is found in a powerful Masonic work published in Germany in 1778.

Gotthold Ephraim Lessing was born in 1729 and died in 1781. He was thus a contemporary of other distinguished Freemasons, such as George Washington and Wolfgang Amadeus Mozart. As a representative of the German Enlightenment he was almost without equal, and his passion for Freemasonry was echoed in a lifelong commitment to its principles. In 1778 he wrote *Ernst und Falk*, a dialogue patterned after Plato's dialogues. Falk is a Freemason and, when the dialogue opens, he is engaged in a conversation with his friend, Ernst, about a variety of subjects. Ernst says to Falk, "Are you a Freemason?" And Falk responds, "I believe myself to be one." The conversation carries on along these lines, with Ernst suggesting that Falk is surely a Freemason because he was obviously initiated in a Masonic lodge. Falk agrees that he was initiated a Mason in a Masonic lodge, but insists that this is not the real reason that he claims to be a Mason. Falk then says, "I believe myself to be a Freemason – not so much for the reason that I was initiated by older Masons in a warranted Lodge, but because I understand and perceive what Freemasonry is and why it is, when and where it came into existence, and by what means it is advanced or retarded." The rest of the dialogues are an expansion of this statement. Ernst is intrigued with what Freemasonry means to Falk, and Falk is glad to explain it.

There is one part of the dialogue that is especially intriguing in our present discussion of Masonic relief. Falk, upon being challenged by Ernst to recount the things that Freemasons do for others – as opposed to doing things for themselves – is treated to a litany of Masonic philanthropies of the day: a foundling hospital in Stockholm, a workhouse for poor young girls in Dresden, a school for poor boys in Brunswick, and a free public

25

school in Berlin. Falk is modest, but Ernst presses him to admit that Freemasons do all this for the publicity they get. Falk vehemently denies this, and says, "The real deeds of the Freemasons are so great, look so far ahead, that whole centuries could pass by before one was able to say, 'That have they done!' Nevertheless, all the good that is still in the world—note well, in the world! – have they done. And they are continuing to work at all the good which will yet be in the world." And then Ernst closes this part of the conversation, with a riddle: "Good deeds...aim at making good deeds superfluous."

Think carefully about the meaning of that riddle as you read about Masonic relief elsewhere in this magazine. Lessing is saying that good deeds are not just done to relieve a temporary distress, but rather to set in motion things that will ultimately make those deeds superfluous. In Lessing's day there were no hospitals for the poor but Freemasons started them, and soon society came to accept its responsibility for medical care for the poor. In Lessing's day there were no widespread public schools but Freemasons created them, and soon society came to accept its responsibility for a free public educational system, open to all. Masonic relief has immediate and valuable results in reaching out to those in need. But Freemasons also work to raise the consciousness of society to effect needed change. Freemasonry believed in equality of men before God, and in 1776 a new political society took its place among the nations of the earth based on Masonic principles. Freemasons founded the Shriners hospitals when children suffered from infantile paralysis. When that dreaded disease had been conquered, they then helped children with other needs.

Freemasonry is thus much more than a relief society, dedicated to doing good works. It is an idea and an ideal—a force for good that changes the world for the better. And it has been doing it for almost three hundred years.

RECOMMENDING A MAN TO BECOME A MASON
The key word is fidelity

By John L. Cooper III
California Freemason, Spring 2003

Before modern Masonry arose at the end of the seventeenth century, the "making of a Mason" was accompanied by reading from the *Old Charges*. These ancient documents contained the history and legends of the craft, and taught the candidate the important teachings of Masonry that had been handed down from time immemorial. Today these are found in the three charges that are delivered to our candidates, one for each degree.

In California, the charge to an Entered Apprentice is found in our *Monitor*, and unlike the secret work, is published for the entire world to see. It ends with this solemn injunction:

> Finally: Be faithful to the trust committed to your care, and manifest your fidelity to your principles by a strict observance of the Constitutions of the Fraternity; by adhering to the Ancient Landmarks thereof; and by refusing to recommend any one to a participation in our privileges, unless you have strong reasons to believe that, by a similar fidelity, he will ultimately reflect honor on our ancient Institution.

The last phrase is the key to what we expect of an Entered Apprentice when it comes to recommending a man to become a Mason. Only a Master Mason can sign an application for another to receive the degrees of Masonry. But, at the very beginning of his Masonic journey, we tell an Entered Apprentice what test he should use when recommending— or even encouraging—anyone else to seek to become a Mason.

The key word is fidelity. Faithfulness to the same things that he has just learned are the important tenets that every Entered Apprentice learned when he was made a Mason.

These tenets are: relying on God as the source of his faith and life; treating his neighbor as he himself wants to be treated; shaping his own life to be of service to others; loving his country and earning the reputation of a good citizen; taking charge of his personal behavior and making himself a better man; and being a man of honesty and honor, always keeping promises that he makes.

These are among the tests of whether a Master Mason should

recommend a man to be made a Mason by signing his application.

Notice that there is nothing about how long we have known a man before we can sign his application. In this day and age, it is likely that a man who asks to become a Mason may not be known to anyone in the lodge.

The question is not how long we have known him, but how much we know about him. We can find it out, if we are willing to do so. This requirement is no barrier to the growth of Masonry; instead it is an impetus to seek out good men, and lead them to seek membership in our fraternity.

Membership in Masonry is and always will be selective, because— in the words of the charge—it is "honorable, as tending to make all me—so who are strictly obedient to its precepts."

THE MASTER AND THE LODGE
A model of Masonic leadership

By John L. Cooper III
California Freemason, Summer 2003

The master of a Masonic lodge is a unique leader. Once elected, he inherits significant powers to rule and govern the members of the lodge. He is invested with time-honored responsibilities that are unlike those of the president of any other society, and he is given unusual authority in the discharge of his duties. Once installed, he cannot be removed by vote of his brethren who elected him. Only a Masonic trial for malfeasance in office, or action by the grand master can take him out of office.

Many organizations have the office of past president, but only serving as the master of a masonic lodge confers unique status as a past master, and then only after having fully discharged the duty laid upon him at his installation. The master of a lodge who resigns, or does not complete his term as master (unless he dies in office) does not become a past master. How did all this come about?

The origin of the office of master of a Masonic lodge is lost in the mists of history, along with the origin of Freemasonry itself. But as far back as we have any record, the office of master existed. In 1717, when the first grand lodge was formed in London, England, the four lodges that formed it placed the oldest Master Mason then present—who was also the master of one of the lodges—in the chair as grand master "pro tem," and then proceeded to elect a grand master.

The Ancients – a rival grand lodge of the original grand lodge of 1717—claimed to preserve the oldest traditions of Freemasonry. With the Ancients, the office of past master was especially esteemed. Among both the Moderns (as the premier grand lodge was called) and the Ancients, the Master Mason degree was originally a qualifying degree for those who wished to become master of the lodge. In fact, the third degree was originally called the master's part because it was designed to instruct the future master in the significant duties of his office. California follows the tradition of the Moderns by allowing a warden to preside over the lodge if the master is not present. However, a warden does not exercise all the rights and powers of the installed master, even in this jurisdiction. Some prerogatives are reserved only to the man who has been elected and installed as master.

What does this say about the master as the leader of the lodge? He is the leader because he was elected and installed as such by his brethren. Once elected and installed, he becomes the master teacher as well as the head of the lodge. He becomes the master workman, the master designer, who sets his lodge at work, and gives them the necessary instruction to do what they are supposed to do as Masons. He has been specially set apart for this work, and having been set apart, he cannot ever truly return to the body of the workmen in the same status as before his election and installation as master.

That is why the rank of past master is considered to be the highest rank within the power of the lodge to grant to one of its members.

Leadership in Freemasonry is thus much more than simply being elected as the presiding officer of a lodge; it is the conferring of a dignity within the order that is unrivaled by any other, except for that of grand master. Indeed, when he becomes master of his lodge, he occupies "the dignified and honorable position to which the suffrage" of his brethren has called him.

Masonic Colleges

By John L. Cooper III
California Freemason, Fall 2003

On a bluff overlooking the Missouri River at Lexington, Mo., there is a monument to a noble endeavor of the Grand Lodge of Missouri during the first half of the nineteenth century. The public memorial commemorates the first Masonic college in the United States – a unique contribution of Freemasonry in the nineteenth century to higher education. At the 1841 Annual Communication of the Grand Lodge of Missouri, Grand Master Stephen Carnegy introduced a resolution for the establishment of a Masonic college for the education of sons of indigent Masons and others. The phrase "and others" meant that the college would serve the public – an important step for the fledgling fraternity on the frontier of the expanding American Republic.

In 1846 the college moved to Lexington, the county seat of Lafayette County and later the scene of an early battle in the Civil War. At the time this ambitious project was undertaken the Grand Lodge of Missouri was only 21 years old and had 1,139 members.

The college taught the curriculum of the day to its students: natural philosophy and astronomy, mathematics, mental and moral science, ancient languages, and literature. Tuition was free to deserving students, funded by the Grand Lodge *per capita*, but students had to pay for their own board and lodging. In 1846 it cost $25 a year for room and board. By 1853 an endowment fund of $53,000 had been raised to support the college and citizens of Lexington had added another $30,000 in donations.

However, this effort was overshadowed by the looming Civil War. In 1859 neighboring Kansas had become a bloody battleground between the proponents of slavery and the abolitionists. In both Kansas and Missouri, guerilla groups terrorized the local population, and had a dampening effect on all efforts at public service. By 1859 the Grand Lodge of Missouri was unable to sustain its effort and the college was closed. The buildings were badly damaged during the Battle of Lexington in 1861.

After the war, Grand Lodge gave the campus to the Marvin Female Institute with the proviso that up to 30 daughters of deceased Masons could attend free of tuition. That college later ceased to function and the site was donated to the City of Lexington, which maintains the memorial in a beautiful city park overlooking the river.

Although Missouri was the first, it was not the only grand lodge to found colleges in the nineteenth century. Kentucky, Ohio, Arkansas, and Georgia also joined the movement. In order to understand why Freemasons undertook this effort, it must be remembered that colleges in America during the first half of the nineteenth century were almost exclusively the provinces of the churches. Primarily intended to prepare young men for the Christian ministry, ill-prepared to meet the educational needs of the secular American society on the frontier.

Freemasonry, with its roots in the Enlightenment, had a belief that education would liberate men and women to become the leaders of the new republic. In a society that would be based on merit, rather than inherited wealth or social status, education was the key that would unlock the door to the future. As always, Freemasons have made a commitment to the future by self-sacrifice in the present. The nineteenth century was no exception, and the Masonic college movement was but one way that Freemasonry contributed to the shaping of the American nation.

St. Lawrence and the Treasures

By John L. Cooper III
California Freemason, Winter 2003

There is a curious Masonic degree called St. Lawrence the Martyr. Many Masonic degrees have a legend or story associated with them, and the Degree of St. Lawrence the Martyr is no exception. And as with many of the additional degrees beyond ancient craft Masonry, this degree is intended to extend the basic teaching about charity by adding a new dimension. In the first degree of Masonry, a candidate is taught the meaning of charity in a powerful and personal way. He learns that no matter how destitute he may find himself, he will never lack as long as one Mason remains alive to help him. And, in a similar manner, he is now bound to extend the same help to any other Mason in need. The Degree of St. Lawrence the Martyr takes this one step further by telling us what charity really means.

In the year 258, a deacon at Rome by the name of Lawrence was arrested. According to legend—the legend that became the Masonic Degree of St. Lawrence the Martyr—the Emperor ordered Lawrence to produce the "treasures" of the church. Knowing that Christians distributed enormous amounts of food and clothing to the poor, the Emperor assumed that this must be made possible because the Christians were enormously wealthy. In fact they were not. Although there were some Christians who were wealthy, the vast majority were poor, and many were slaves who owned no property at all. What was the source of this great charity? It was sacrificial giving on the part of all members, rich and poor, who gave without asking for anything in return. Lawrence knew this and the Emperor did not.

The Emperor gave Lawrence three days to produce the treasures of the church. Three days later he did. He filled the streets of Rome with thousands and thousands of poor people who came out in droves to demonstrate how many were helping one another through this primitive system of charity. The Emperor, angered at being mocked, ordered Lawrence to be roasted alive.

In subsequent centuries he became St. Lawrence, with churches named after him, and even a Masonic degree using his story to teach a lesson in charity. What is that lesson? That our true treasures are people, and not things. True charitable giving is giving without any expectation of receiving anything in return. We do not enrich others by our giving—we enrich ourselves. We become the treasures not because we have great wealth, but because we understand that giving to others makes us rich.

Lawrence's treasures were not the wealthy who gave to the poor— they were the poor who shared what they had with others. It is the principle of caring. And it is no surprise that "charity" comes from the Latin word for "caring"—*caritas*. Our Masonic trilogy might also be translated as "faith, hope, and caring"—because that is really what charity is all about.

MORAL ARCHITECTURE

By John L. Cooper III
California Freemason, Spring 2004

Freemasonry sometimes takes surprising turns as it unfolds its beauties to a candidate. Just when he thinks he has figured out the general direction of a train of thought, he is taken in a different, sometimes startling, direction. So it is when a Fellow Craft Mason hears for the first time the interest that Freemasons have in architecture.

As an Entered Apprentice he is introduced to the idea that he is building a spiritual house—a house "not made with hands, eternal in the heavens."

He is symbolically placed close to the master of the lodge when he reenters it as a newly made Entered Apprentice Mason, and is told that he is thus placed so that he will learn how to build his "future moral and Masonic edifice." For the first time he is told of the connection between architecture and morality—a theme pervasive in Freemasonry.

In the lecture of the Fellow Craft degree, the candidate is told that Freemasonry consists of two fundamental concepts: operative Masonry and speculative Masonry. Initially, the candidate is led to conclude that in olden times Masons built physical buildings, whereas in modern times they build philosophical structures.

The lecture then goes on to describe some things about the way in which operative Masons build when he is told that this kind of Masonry is concerned with the "proper application of the useful rules of architecture, whence a structure will derive figure, strength, and beauty and from which will result a due proportion and just correspondence in all its parts."

After explaining how such knowledge is necessary for the building of physical structures, he is then told that today Masons build nonmaterial structures by shaping the material of their lives into something as useful as the physical buildings which shelter us from the inclemencies of the weather. A "speculative" Mason is to subdue his passions, act upon the square, keep a tongue of good report, maintain secrecy, and practice charity.

This brief introduction is followed by a more lengthy discussion of architecture itself, and especially classical architecture, with its emphasis on symmetry and order, upon form and beauty. Teaching again by induction, the lectures do not tell the candidate that this applies to what he is building within himself. And all too frequently the candidate passes over this curious bit of reference to antique architecture without discovering how much it has to teach him about his own "moral and masonic edifice."

Masons of the seventeenth and eighteenth centuries were fascinated by classical architecture—the architecture of ancient Greece and Rome. They contrasted the principles of this type of architecture with those of the Middle Ages—the so-called "Gothic" architecture that was so different. They found Gothic architecture to be flawed because it had none of the symmetry and order which so impressed them in the architecture of Greece and Rome. The model they took for the ideal was the classical model, and hence its explanation in the lecture of the Fellow Craft degree.

Without understanding why classical architecture was so important to those who created our lectures, we cannot truly understand what they were trying to tell us. And as a result, much of the lesson is easily missed. As an example, take the five orders of architecture.

The Senior Deacon explains to the candidate that the "ancient and original orders of architecture, esteemed by Masons, are no more than three, the Doric, Ionic, and Corinthian, which were invented by the Greeks. To these the Romans added two, the Tuscan, which they made plainer than the Doric, and the Composite, which was more ornamental, if not more beautiful than the Corinthian."

These are presented to the candidate, but nothing is said as to why they are important to him as a Mason. If he is perceptive, he must be puzzled, because he was earlier told that Masons today are philosophical (speculative), and surely this bit of information pertains to operative Masonry.

Unless the candidate is professionally an architect, or intends on becoming one, this bit of information is surely not very useful. Or is it?

Is there something hidden here for the candidate to learn by induction? Is he expected to take this information and apply it to the construction of his "moral and masonic edifice"? I believe that there is, and here is a meaning to consider.

Classical architecture is classified into categories by the types of columns that supported as well as decorated the building. Although the Romans were familiar with the arch, they generally used it only in utilitarian architecture, such as aqueducts. Temples and other public buildings followed the traditional means of supporting the roof by a series of closely spaced pillars or columns. And the Romans followed the Greeks in creating a sense of order and beauty by carving all the columns of a building in a similar manner.

The earliest buildings used the simple technique of fluting of columns to make them seem slim and graceful, despite the sturdiness needed to hold up the great weight of the stone roof. To keep the columns from sinking into the ground—or punching through the roof—they developed the concept of "caps"—capitals — on the columns. The way in which these capitals were carved determined the orders in architecture to which our lectures refer. The simplest is no capital at all, or only a rudimentary one—the Tuscan—which, although a late development, took simplicity to one extreme.

The most ornate of the three types was the Corinthian—a capital decorated with acanthus leaves, making the column to appear as if it were a living, growing support for the building. The Doric added a plain capital, and the Ionic added a scroll-like carving to the primitive capital. The Composite, in turn, blended the acanthus leaves of the Corinthian with the scroll-like capital of the Ionic. In this manner classical architecture came to understand the five orders in architecture.

Is there any symbolic meaning here for a Mason? I think that there is. Our "moral and masonic edifice"—our lives that we are building—are in reality supported by symbolic columns that raise our effort toward the heavens. There is an understanding that if what we build remains low and unimposing, it will never inspire any others to imitate what we have built. But by raising the superstructure on columns of beauty as well as utility, our moral and masonic edifice soars into the sky.

We choose the style in which we build, but all have an equal value, for all hold up the superstructure. Our understanding of life may be of the simplest variety—Tuscan, if you will. We may not have the talents with which others are blessed, but we can build well nonetheless.

On the other hand, others may build with great simplicity but also with great symmetry. Their lives are marked by consistency and order. They are the Doric and Ionic columns—simple, honest, but also with a beauty of their own. Others may achieve great things in life—sometimes many great things—symbolized by the Corinthian and the Composite.

But all of us share the same values, the same understanding of Freemasonry, regardless of which order in architecture we use to erect our moral and masonic edifice. We are all "friends and brothers, among whom there should be no contention, but that noble contention, or rather emulation, of who best can work and best agree."

One definition of Freemasonry is that it is "moral architecture." If so, then one of the beautiful lessons we learn from the five orders of architecture is that diversity in how we build is of immense value. We are not all of the same religion — or the same race — or the same language. But we all erect buildings of superb beauty, according to our understanding of the art. We truly are engaged in building that "house not made with hands, eternal in the heavens."

Freemasonry and the Initiatic Process

By John L. Cooper III
California Freemason, Summer 2004

In common Masonic parlance, a Mason is initiated, passed, and raised—he is initiated an Entered Apprentice Mason, passed to the degree of Fellow Craft, and raised to the sublime degree of Master Mason. Yet it is not in the first degree alone that a Mason experiences initiation.

There are multiple initiations as a Mason moves from stage to stage within a degree, and from degree to degree as the mysteries of Freemasonry are unfolded to him. Thus Freemasonry may be properly termed an initiatic brotherhood, a system of progressive revelation of information that helps the Mason to understand more than he knew before at each step of the journey.

But because this Masonic initiatic experience has settled down over the last few centuries into a series of degrees, we often confuse the taking of a degree with true participation in the initiatic process itself. Such, however, is not the case.

Initiation is not an external and physical activity; it is an internal and spiritual activity for which the framework of a degree or of many degrees serves as a pathway. A Mason may take all the degrees of Freemasonry available to him and never experience a spiritual initiation. A non-Mason may never take any of the degrees of Freemasonry, and yet experience a spiritual initiation akin to what Freemasonry is intended to accomplish through study and meditation on the same teachings that Freemasonry organizes into its degrees. In fact, Freemasons have long recognized this truth, referring to individuals who, for whatever reason, are not or cannot be Freemasons under our prevailing rules—as "Masons without the apron." Their Freemasonry derives not from receiving the degrees of Masonry in the traditional manner, but from having conformed their lives to the teachings of Freemasonry, and having passed through the same kind of spiritual experience that the degrees are intended to foster.

This subject is of more than academic interest. A debate often takes place between those committed to our traditional way of making Masons and those who believe that there are alternate ways of making Masons.

When the initiatic process is properly understood, the arguments are not really opposed to one another. Each is insisting on the validity of the initiatic process as a means of becoming a Mason. If they each laid their arguments side by side, they would find remarkable agreement on the nature of the initiatic process and how one becomes a Freemason.

The initiatic process actually starts long before a man knocks at the door of a Masonic lodge. In some old rituals a Mason is asked where he was first prepared to be made a Mason, and he replies, "In my heart." And that is true.

Unless an individual is prepared in his heart to become a Mason— unless he has prepared himself to be open to learning what Freemasonry has to teach him—the degrees of Masonry will make little impact on him. The monitorial marshal's questions, asked of a candidate before he is allowed to knock at the door of the lodge, state it clearly: "Do you seriously declare, upon your honor, that unbiased by friends and uninfluenced by mercenary motives, you freely and voluntarily offer yourself as a candidate for the mysteries of Masonry?" A candidate must be ready to learn in order to be truly prepared for what he will experience through the mysteries of Masonry.

Our degrees nowadays are laid out in sections. Although we require certain proficiency between the degrees, there is initiatic progression within each degree between the sections of which no proficiency is required. That does not mean that we have no expectation that the candidate will ever become proficient—become knowledgeable—about the meaning of the several ceremonies which occur within a single degree. We do expect him to work on becoming knowledgeable about the experience through a lifetime of learning about the meaning of those ceremonies.

And that is true for all the degrees of Masonry, regardless of how much we require him to memorize and recite in lodge between the degrees. The old long form proficiencies were never intended to teach the candidate all that there is to know about the preceding degree, and neither are the newer short form proficiencies.

They are both intended to whet his appetite for returning again and again to what he has experienced, making his initiatic experience the work of a lifetime.

The process is much greater than the conferral of the degrees themselves.

Initiation is a process that goes on continuously. It does not begin when a candidate knocks at the door of a lodge, but rather it begins when he first seeks out the light that Masonry has to offer. It does not occur because he takes a degree, or even if he takes a degree and memorizes some ritual pertaining to that degree. It occurs because his mind and spirit absorb the meaning of the teachings unfolded to him through the initiatic process. And it keeps on occurring throughout his life, if he rightly understands it, until at last he lays down his working tools for the final time.

Initiation is not merely a beginning. It is a series of beginnings that occurs many times in a single degree, and many times as various rites and degrees unfold new vistas to his understanding. It is also not necessarily linear. Progressive does not always imply forward movement in one direction. It can mean a deeper understanding of truths previously understood, but understood in a new context as the years go by.

Freemasonry is a progressive moral science not because it consists of a series of degrees, but because it consists of a series of experiences that causes us to think through the meaning of life in light of its teachings. Freemasonry is an initiatic fraternity not because it confers three degrees on three separate nights, but because it brings a man into contact with a fresh understanding of ultimate reality through a series of steps.

In the final analysis, it is not whether a Mason became one in a single day, a single year, or a single decade. It is whether he becomes a Mason through a lifetime of initiation.

Manifest Destiny and Freemasonry

By John L. Cooper III
California Freemason, Fall 2004

Most historians agree that the United States of America was a unique experiment at its beginning, and continued to exhibit unusual characteristics throughout its history, even to the present time. Although history records not a few republics or states that had no monarch, only the United States emerged on the stage of history as a republic composed of individual republics. And only the United States, of all countries in the world, set out to establish its empire by creating self-governing, self-sustaining republics as it grew into its manhood.

Beginning with thirteen original and sovereign political units when independence from Great Britain was declared in 1776, by 1787 these original English colonies had formed the world's first republic within a republic—a federation of individual republics, or states, which had irrevocably bound themselves together into a federal union called the United States of America.

Freemasonry in the United States mirrored this unique political creation. An abortive attempt to create a national grand lodge, with George Washington as its first general Grand Master, did not succeed. And just as new republics were admitted to the Union as they were organized as political territories of the expanding nation, so each of these units formed its own Masonic grand lodge.

Sovereignty was surrendered by the United States to each of its new states as they were created, and grand lodges similarly surrendered sovereignty over their lodges in the expanding territories as new—and equal—grand lodges were formed. Today there are 51 Masonic grand lodges in the United States, something that could not have happened had it not been for the unique American political experiment of creating sovereign states as it expanded westward.

The expansion of the United States to the Pacific shore is sometimes called Manifest Destiny. Many Americans in the nineteenth century believed that it was a God-given destiny that the United States should eventually rule the portion of North America from the Atlantic Ocean to the Pacific Ocean. Later pared down by the realities that both Canada and Mexico would not allow the United States to frustrate their own national ambitions, we settled for the idea that the middle of the North American continent should be forever the United States of America.

Following the political development of this vast territory, Freemasonry spread along with the pioneers into the American West—an active agent that made the American dream of one nation stretching from coast to coast a reality.

Wherever Americans settled, they founded Masonic lodges—and eventually grand lodges as well. The American doctrine of territorial exclusivity maintained that whenever at least three lodges in a territory came into existence they could abandon their allegiance to the grand lodge which chartered them, and take out a new charter from a grand lodge newly formed in the territory or state.

Thus each new territory became a grand lodge in due course—except for California, which did not pass through the state of an organized territory before being admitted as a state in the American Union on September 9, 1850. The Grand Lodge of California was formed on April 19 of that same year—older by a few months than the state itself.

What role did Freemasonry play on the American frontier? Wherever Americans settled they quickly formed Masonic lodges. As indicated above, they also quickly formed grand lodges—independent governing units of Freemasonry in the growing nation. As lodges were mostly self-governing, so these new grand lodges were also self-governing. They reflected the new self-government of the territories, and eventually, of the states that followed. As Freemasonry had provided a matrix in which the original colonies had learned the virtues of self-government, so Freemasonry provided a model of self-government for the territories that eventually became a part of the American Union.

Democracy spread across the continent as Freemasonry spread across this same land mass. And everywhere Americans staked out their right to govern themselves in this new land—as did Freemasons as well.

Freemasonry and Manifest Destiny were intertwined as the American republic expanded from shore to shore. Our political experiment was unique, as was our Masonic experiment. The idea of local sovereignty was implicit in the way in which the United States grew to maturity. And the idea of the sovereignty of each grand lodge was also implicit in our understanding that lodges could leave behind their original allegiance, and form a new allegiance to a grand lodge in the emerging state in which it was located.

Freemasonry was changed by the American experience of Manifest Destiny. And the American experience of local self-government was, in turn, heavily influenced by the successful expansion of Freemasonry on the frontier as new grand lodges took their equal place with the grand lodges of the states that went before them.

ANTI-MASONRY THROUGH THE CENTURIES

By John L. Cooper III
California Freemason, Winter 2004

Freemasonry has attracted opponents from early in its history. An act of the English Parliament in 1425 was very clear:

> Whereas by yearly Congregations and Confederacies, made by the Masons in their General Assemblies, the good Course and Effect of the Statutes of Laborers be openly violated and broken in Subversion of the Law and to the great Damage of all the Commons, our said Sovereign Lord the King, willing in this case to provide a Remedy, by the Advice and Assent aforesaid, and at the special Request of the Commons, hath ordained and established, that such Chapters and Congregations shall not be hereafter holden; and if any such be made, they that cause such Chapters and Congregations to be assembled and holden, if they thereof be convicted, shall be judged Felons, and that the other Masons that come to such Chapters and Congregations be punished by Imprisonment of their Bodies, and make Fine and Ransome at the king's Will. (Act 3, Henry VI, Ch. 1)

In this case, our operative ancestors were "combining in restraint of trade" by refusing to work except for a minimum wage—an act which was against the law in those days.

Nineteen years before the formation of the first grand lodge in 1717, a pamphlet appeared in the streets of London attacking Freemasonry as being a devilish sect of men, evil-doers, and corrupt people. The pamphlet further warned, "take care lest their Ceremonies and Swearings take hold of you; and be wary that none cause you to err from Godliness." The pamphlet was probably a sermon, printed for distribution.

The organization of the first grand lodge did nothing to stop attacks on Freemasonry. However, the decades after 1717 saw ridicule added to the attacks on the craft. Masons themselves sometimes joined in holding up the fraternity to ridicule—especially when the actions of some Masons earned it. William Hogarth, for example, was a member of the lodge that met at the Hand and Apple Tree Tavern in Little Queen Street, London, and was grand steward in 1735. Nevertheless, Hogarth published engravings that poked fun at the drunken activities of some lodges at the time. His famous engraving, "Night," shows the master of a Masonic lodge walking home at night through the streets of London, accompanied by his tiler. Both are evidently quite drunk, and are raising a row as they go through the streets singing at the top of their lungs—much to the displeasure of the neighborhood. One disgruntled matron is shown emptying the contents of a chamber pot out her second-story window onto them!

Some anti-Masonry results from a misunderstanding of Freemasonry, some from jealousy of those who are not members, and some from political regimes who are intolerant of those who are not under their control. But some anti-Masonry results directly from our own actions as Masons and our inability to explain Freemasonry to the world at large. There is little we can do about the former, but much we can do about the latter. Our own behavior as Freemasons must always be beyond reproach. The avoidance of scandal starts with a commitment to always doing what we know to be right—without compromise. In addition, we can become well informed about Freemasonry so that we can explain it to others, whether to family and friends, or to the society in which we live.

We do have secret signs, tokens and words by which we are known to one another, but we are not a secret society. Masonic secrecy comes from how Freemasonry is taught—a progressive moral discipline, revealed to its initiates by steps, or degrees. Masonic secrecy has nothing to do with hiding anything from non-Masons that we do not wish the world to know.

Our principles and our teachings are, and should be, public. How we communicate those principles and teachings forms the basis of our secret work—the ritual through which Freemasonry is taught. We owe no apology or explanation to the world for this fact. It is a part of what we are. But we should never shy away from telling the story of Freemasonry openly to others. Light is an important Masonic symbol, and it is an important privilege and duty to share the light of Freemasonry with others.

THE ROYAL ART

By John L. Cooper III
California Freemason, Spring 2005

In an issue of the *California Freemason* devoted to the subject of art, it is particularly interesting to take a look at how the term "art" is used in Freemasonry and its rituals. Three times in the progress toward becoming a Master Mason, the candidate hears a mysterious phrase repeated to him. He is told that he is to hold as of great importance the "arts, parts, or points of the hidden mysteries of Freemasonry." No further explanation is given him as to what this phrase means.

According to *Webster's Unabridged Dictionary*, the word "art" comes from the Latin word for "to join," as in to join things together—to arrange them. An arrangement is made up of its parts, and in some sense the word art means the whole of something—an arrangement of all its parts—as opposed to its several distinct parts.

In the phrase, "the arts, parts, or points of the hidden mysteries of Freemasonry" we may well understand that we are to look to the whole of Freemasonry, as well as to its several parts. In order to understand the entirety of something, we must be able to understand the parts of which it is made. And in order to understand how the parts fit together we must see the whole picture as well.

I am reminded of the story of the four blind men and the elephant. One grasped its tail, and said that the elephant was like a rope. Another grasped its ear, and said that it was like a great leaf. Another grasped its trunk, and said an elephant was like a snake. And finally, another, leaning against the great side of the elephant said that all the others were wrong. It was surely like the wall of a house. All were right. And all were wrong.

The introduction of this phrase at an important point in our progress through the hidden mysteries of Freemasonry may be intended to teach us to understand this lesson. We cannot know the whole of Freemasonry unless we understand its several parts. And if we think of a particular part of Freemasonry as the whole of Freemasonry, then we also miss the point. We pledge ourselves to an entire understanding of Freemasonry when we repeat these important phrases.

The blue lodge is the foundation of Freemasonry, but it is not the whole of Masonry. This year the grand master has reminded us of the importance of the family of Freemasonry. Organizations which are composed of Masons, of Masons and their family members, or which are based on the principles of Freemasonry, are all an expression of Freemasonry.

Just because the core of Freemasonry is found in the three basic degrees of Entered Apprentice, Fellow Craft, and Master Mason, we should not make the mistake of thinking that this is the whole of Freemasonry. The York Rite, the Scottish Rite, the Shrine, Order of the Eastern Star, DeMolay, Job's Daughters, Rainbow Girls, and many more organizations whose members are Freemasons, whose members are related to Freemasons, or whose principles are inspired by Freemasonry, make up the whole of Freemasonry.

This curious phase, introduced to a Mason at an important point in the ritual, the "arts, parts, and points of the hidden mysteries of Freemasonry," teaches a very important lesson. The art of Freemasonry is the kaleidoscope of systems and organizations, of degrees and rituals, in many different countries and many different languages, which make up the arrangement of that "beautiful system of morality, veiled in allegory, and illustrated by symbol."

THE THREE STEPS USUALLY DELINEATED UPON THE MASTER'S CARPET

By John L. Cooper III
California Freemason, Summer 2005

The long form of the lecture of the third degree is heard infrequently in most California lodges, yet it has some of the most important symbolism of all the degrees. When the long form is not given as a part of the degree, the candidate is advised to study the symbolism in the *Monitor*—a "textbook" of Freemasonry—that he will soon receive. Some newly raised Master Masons do take a look at the *Monitor*, but many do not and therefore miss the explanation of the symbols of the third degree handed down from early times.

One such symbol is The Three Steps, and we are told that it is usually delineated upon the master's carpet. Since a carpet assigned to the master of the lodge fell into disuse many years ago, it is no use looking for The Three Steps on any carpet in the east. A remnant of this symbol, however, is still to be found in the architectural detail of many lodge rooms. The perceptive candidate will note that the junior warden's station is elevated by one step, the senior warden's by two steps, and the master's station by three. This architectural detail is now all that remains of a once-powerful symbol of our Masonic teaching about youth, manhood, and old age.

Many symbols of Freemasonry overlap one another due to accidents of history. The stations of the three principal officers of the lodge are but one example. Because we hear it more frequently at the opening of a lodge, we are used to the idea that the east represents the morning of life, the south, the noon of life, and the west, the evening of life. Those symbols are important, and in many lodge rooms are augmented by representations of the sun rising in the east, at meridian height in the south, and setting in the west. But this symbolism is not the same as The Three Steps, or rather three sets of steps—one in the south, two in the west, and three in the east. It is this symbolism that is reflected in the monitorial work in the lecture of the third degree. And because this symbolism is less obvious, it is often missed. It should not be: It is a beautiful symbol worth exploring.

These steps are associated in the ritual with the three degrees of ancient craft Masonry. Youth is likened to the Entered Apprentice degree, manhood to the Fellow Craft degree, and age to the Master Mason degree. We are then told that in youth we are to "industriously occupy our minds in the attainments of useful knowledge." As Fellow Crafts we are to "apply our knowledge to the discharge of our respective duties to God, our neighbors, and ourselves." Then—as Master Masons—we "may enjoy the happy reflection consequent on a well-spent life."

This issue of *California Freemason* is devoted to youth. As such, it is worth reflecting on what Freemasonry says about youth in its ritual. The most obvious place is the symbolism of "The Three Steps usually delineated upon the master's carpet"—or nowadays represented by the single step leading to the junior warden's station. The junior warden's station thus becomes the place in the lodge devoted symbolically to "industry"—what we today would call hard work. But it is not hard work for hard work's sake. It is hard work aimed at obtaining useful knowledge. Freemasonry is in some sense a journey in search of truth, but truth must emerge from a base of knowledge. Unless we work hard to obtain knowledge at the beginning of our journey, the rest of the trip will be far more difficult—or even fruitless.

One cannot apply knowledge that one does not possess. The symbolism of The Three Steps is that we have to do "first things first." First comes knowledge, and then comes usefulness to God, our neighbors, and ourselves. The important thing is not whether or not we take this first step in our actual youth—in fact, many people do not take this first step until late in life. But all must take it. Each individual must go through the symbolic progression of youth, manhood, and age—no matter when he starts. If you have not yet started to attain that knowledge of life and of Masonry, why not start now?

Freemasonry and the Victorian Era: An Overview

By John L. Cooper III
California Freemason, Fall 2005

It should come as no surprise that an institution such as Freemasonry should be influenced by the times in which it exists. Nevertheless, we are conditioned to think of Freemasonry as something unchanged over time. Even our ritual leads us to this mistaken conclusion. In the *Monitor*, adopted by the Masonic Grand Lodge of California as a textbook, we read that "Freemasonry, notwithstanding, has still survived. ... Tools and implements of architecture most expressive are selected by the fraternity to imprint upon the memory wise and serious truths; and thus, through the succession of ages, are transmitted unimpaired the most excellent tenets of our institution."

In a certain sense, of course, this is true. The forms and rituals of Freemasonry are very old, and we can discern the outline of our present degrees in materials that have been in use for at least the last three centuries. However, this often leads us to the erroneous conclusion that Freemasonry has remained unchanged over the years. And even more inaccurate is the notion that Freemasonry has held itself aloof from the societies in which it has existed. The fact is that Freemasonry as an institution has always been influenced by contemporary society, and the shape of the institution has been molded by the ideas and fashions of particular places and times.

In many ways, the Masonry of the Victorian Era (1837–1901) provides a perfect snapshot of how the craft has been shaped by the historical forces prevailing at a particular time in history—and at the same time how Masonry has had a profound effect on society at large.

Modern Freemasonry is in many respects the product of the Victorian Era. In those days not only was Freemasonry very influential in shaping society, but membership in a Masonic lodge was part and parcel of being part of the intellectual and political elite. When Victoria ascended the throne in 1837, her cousin, the Duke of Sussex (son of George III), was grand master of the United Grand Lodge of England. Her son Edward was grand master of the United Grand Lodge until shortly before he was crowned as King Edward VII. Queen Victoria herself allowed the grand lodge to award her the title of Protectoress of Freemasonry. Most of the prominent decision makers in Queen Victoria's government were Freemasons, and the close relationship between the leaders in Victorian England and Freemasonry is a well-established fact. Two books by Dr. Paul

Rich, *Elixir of Empire* and *Chains of Empire*, are well worth reading, not only for their explanation of how the "old boy" network within the British Empire functioned, but also because they provide detailed information about the Masonic component in that network.

Of course, the craft's close association with the royal family in Victorian England had its disadvantages, as well. The story of Jack the Ripper gripped Victorian-era London in no small part because of the various conspiracy theories that put the royal family and the Freemasons at the center of a savage and gruesome murder plot. Of course, the only reason that these rumors gained credence in the first place was because of the close association of Freemasonry with the royal family, which continues to this day. Victoria's son, as we have already learned, was grand master before becoming King, as was his grandson, King George VI. Queen Elizabeth's husband, Prince Philip, Duke of Edinburgh, is a Master Mason, and the current grand master of the United Grand Lodge of England, the Duke of Kent, is the Queen's cousin.

Another relic of Victorian-era Masonry is something that most Freemasons know very little about: the Red Cross of Constantine. There are several local chapters—called conclaves—of this organization in California, and they generally consist of the most active and prominent Masons in the state. The president of the California Masonic Foundation, Most Worshipful M. William Holsinger, is the head of the Los Angeles chapter of this organization, and Past Grand Master R. Stephen Doan is a former presiding officer of this organization, as are other past grand masters. And our grand master himself is in the progressive line to become the sovereign of St. Gabriel's Conclave a few years from now. The Red Cross of Constantine was born during the Victorian Era, and was an outgrowth of an interest in reviving some old traditions and rituals in Freemasonry in London in the 1860s. From this same source came the Masonic Rosicrucian Society, a still-extant organization which has attracted some of the most prominent leaders in Freemasonry. The creation of the Red Cross of Constantine and the Masonic Rosicrucian Society was the result of the work undertaken by Robert Wentworth Little in London in the 1860's.

In many ways, the Victorian era in Britain was the golden age of Masonry. Not only was it *de rigueur* for prominent members of society to be involved, but the importance of the craft was palpable throughout the highest levels of government and business. It is therefore hardly surprising that many of today's Masonic traditions trace their roots back to the standards and practices of that age. At the same time, today's Freemasons have built upon the proud traditions of earlier brothers to reflect the issues and realities that confront the world in the new millennium. Far from being a static organization, Masonry continues to be a dynamic vessel through which our common values can be shared with the world.

INTERIOR ILLUMINATION AND EXTERIOR BRIGHTNESS

By John L. Cooper III
California Freemason, Winter 2006

Freemasonry is understood to be, in part, the science of interior illumination. Our ritual is filled with the symbolism of light and of the progress that a candidate makes as he moves from darkness to light. "Light" for Freemasons stands for knowledge, and for intellectual and psychological development as each Freemason pursues "further light in Masonry." A candidate enters the world of Freemasonry in a symbolic state of darkness—and receives symbolic illumination only after he has taken a solemn obligation which will forever set him apart from the world outside Freemasonry. Our ritual quotes one of the oldest of written documents—the Book of Genesis—moments before a new Mason receives his first light as an Entered Apprentice Mason. Here is what he hears:

> In the beginning God created the heaven and the earth. And the earth was without form, and void; and darkness was upon the face of the deep. And the spirit of God moved upon the face of the waters. And God said, 'Let there be light'; and there was light. (Genesis 1:1–3)

Thus, at the very beginning of his journey as a new Mason, a candidate is taught to seek the light of understanding as found in the source of our being—in God Himself. Whatever his religious persuasion, he is taught that the light he will seek in Freemasonry is but a reflection of the much greater light which God gave humankind from the very beginning. Freemasonry is not a religion itself, but it most emphatically points a Freemason toward the light which is outside of, and beyond, himself. And he must find that light himself. Freemasonry cannot give him the light; it can only encourage him to seek it.

But Freemasonry is not only concerned with interior illumination, and certainly not concerned with interior illumination for its own sake. Every lodge of Free and Accepted Masons is closed with prayer—and that prayer asks that God will give each Mason the vision and the courage to "practice out of the lodge those great moral duties which are inculcated in it..." Freemasonry thus expects a Mason to take the light which he seeks for himself into the world to which he returns when the lodge is closed.

While Freemasonry is concerned with self-illumination, it is more

53

concerned with what a Mason does with that self-illumination. If it serves only to foster interior growth for the Mason himself, it has little value for the larger world in which a Mason lives each day. We expect the search for interior illumination to make a difference in a Mason as he grows in knowledge and understanding—but we expect much more that he will use that knowledge and understanding to make a difference in his family, his community, his country, and his world.

By the time you read this column, many of you will have attended the installation of your lodge. If so, you heard words which express our understanding of the foregoing in the instructions given to the Master as he is installed as a leader of Freemasonry for the twelve months ensuing. The Master is told that he is to "spread and communicate light and instruction to the brethren of [his] lodge." He is further told that he should "Forcibly impress upon them the dignity and high importance of Masonry, and seriously admonish them never to disgrace it." Then he is told that he is to "Charge them to practice out of the lodge those duties which they have been taught in it, and by amiable, discreet, and virtuous conduct, to convince mankind of the goodness of this institution..." Those are powerful words, and they clearly demonstrate that Freemasonry expects its members to carry Freemasonry from the lodge out into the world. This issue is devoted to Freemasonry and the community. The articles tell of the many things that Freemasons do to make their communities a better place for everyone. And now we know why this is so. Freemasonry expects each Mason to transform his interior illumination into an exterior brightness—a brightness that makes the world a better place because a Freemason passed that way.

LET HARMONY PREVAIL

By John L. Cooper
California Freemason, Spring 2006

When the organist of a Masonic lodge in California is installed, the installing officer gives him the following charge:

> The Lyre is the Jewel of your office, and as it is an emblem of music, it should continually remind us that as harmony is essential in the liberal art and science which it symbolizes, so should harmony continue to be the strength and support of all societies, especially of ours. Let harmony prevail!

This charge is peculiar in that it is framed in the context of a prayer. The meaning of the charge in plain English is that as harmony is a dominant theme in music, so should harmony be the dominant theme in a Masonic lodge. The encyclopedia defines harmony as follows:

> Harmony is the use and study of pitch simultaneity and chords, actual or implied, in music. It is sometimes referred to as the 'vertical' aspect of music, with melody being the 'horizontal' aspect.

The phrase "pitch simultaneity" may seem like an arcane and difficult phrase, but it is not really so difficult to understand when we take a look at its meaning in the encyclopedia:

> Simultaneity is the property of two events happening at the same time in at least one reference frame.

What all this means is that harmony is the blending of separate entities into a new entity, without having destroyed the component parts. A musical chord is an example. A chord is three or more notes of different pitches sounding at the same time, and which are perceived by the listener as one musical experience. The image thus created for us of "harmony" is one in which multiple notes or sounds are so played that they seem to be one sound, even though made up of several.

There is a very definite Masonic teaching here. A lodge of Master Masons consists, according to our ritual, of "three or more" Master

Masons. A master's lodge is—or ought to be—a blending of three or more individual Masons who together produce a simultaneous expression of Masonry without having surrendered the individuality of each of those who comprise the lodge. A Masonic lodge is not the suppression of all viewpoints in favor of one. It is the bringing together of diverse viewpoints into one harmonious arrangement in which the beauty of Masonry is expressed. As one note in music by itself does not have the power and beauty of a musical chord, so one Mason alone does not have the power and beauty of Masonry as expressed through his lodge. A Mason can be a Mason in solitude, but the power and beauty of Masonry are much less in solitude than in the harmonious expression of Masonry in the lodge.

Of course, some Masons, and some lodges, have missed this important Masonic teaching. Some Masons come to lodge to make their viewpoints prevail over all others. Some Masons stay away from lodge because they are unable to make their viewpoints prevail over all others. And both groups of Masons miss the point. Masonry is the harmony of all our viewpoints displayed only when we come together as Masons. When we understand this, we get a glimpse as to why, at the opening of every Masonic lodge, we are told that "harmony is the strength and support of all societies—especially of ours." Of all people in the world, Masons should understand this best. In the words of our Installation Ceremony, "Let harmony prevail!

A Progressive Moral Science Divided Into Different Degrees

By John L. Cooper III
California Freemason, Summer 2006

The Fellow Craft degree is one of the more ignored degrees in Freemasonry. Sandwiched as it is between the beginning of the Masonic journey in the Entered Apprentice degree and the powerful Master Mason degree, it is often thought of as less important than the other two—something simply to "pass through" on our way to more important subjects. In fact, we use the term "passed to the degree of Fellow Craft Mason" as descriptive of this phase of our Masonic journey, perhaps without realizing how the use of that term influences our characterization of that degree. However, the degree itself is one of the most powerful expressions of Freemasonry that we possess, and an examination of what it teaches is a fitting preface to an issue of the *California Freemason* magazine devoted to "Masonic Formation," of which more later.

There are two places in the degree where the candidate learns for the first time a real definition of Freemasonry itself. One is the charge at the end of the degree, when he is reminded that "Masonry is a progressive moral science, divided into different degrees..." He is further told that "... as its principles and mystic ceremonies are regularly developed and illustrated, it is intended and hoped that they will make a deep and lasting impression upon your mind." The way in which Freemasonry does this is by bringing the candidate into the presence of profound and significant truths which it expects him to appropriate to himself. It is this which distinguishes the degrees of Freemasonry from mere induction ceremonies common in many fraternal organizations. While these may contain some observations of interest, and even some value as reminding a person of the importance of adhering to certain principles in life, only Freemasonry has as a primary focus the imprinting on the mind of the candidate life-changing ideas which will require a lifetime of study and practice to truly understand.

An acknowledgement of this truth leads to two further observations. First, becoming a Mason is a process rather than an event. Secondly, it must progress in stages if it is to become a permanent characteristic. That is why Masons often speak of Freemasonry as a journey—a journey that begins when he first is attracted to the fraternity and which ends only when he lays down his working tools for the final time. Indeed, common parlance acknowledges this characteristic of Freemasonry. A common greeting between two Masons is often some variant of "I see that you have traveled" or "I see that you are a traveling man." While this is not ritual, nor has it any official meaning, it acknowledges that one Mason can know another not by the pins and rings that he wears, but by a chief characteristic. And while this may, in some sense, reveal a shared image from our ritual, or even acknowledge a poignant moment when a Mason learns that his life's journey may be over a "rough and rugged road," it also acknowledges that Freemasonry is, above all, a journey.

In addition, the concept of a journey in Freemasonry implies that there will be places where we stop in our travels to refresh ourselves and to absorb additional teachings that will help us along our way. That is the meaning of "stages," or "degrees," in Masonry. They are places in our journey where we pause to learn something new, to reflect upon what we have found, and to demonstrate that we understand what we have learned so that we can resume our journey with confidence. It is not so important how long these pauses in our journey are as it is that we take the time to stop and learn at each stage. An essential part of each degree is a question asked of the candidate: "Have you learned what you needed to learn from your previous stop along the way so that you are ready to learn more?" "Have you become proficient enough in what we previously taught you so that now you can take this next step?" Implied in this question is the statement, "If not, go back and work some more. When you are proficient, return to this place and then you can advance. But before we can teach you more, you have to show us that you understand what you learned at your last stopping place." That is a dramatic and ritualistic way of telling the candidate that "Masonry is a progressive moral science, divided into different degrees." It further emphasizes that it is a progressive moral science taught by degrees only. We have no other way of teaching. You have to learn what we taught you before if you are to truly appreciate what we will teach you at this next stage in your Masonic journey.

As a Mason progresses along this journey—this path of life—he is not alone. As an Entered Apprentice he learned that God would be his guide through life, although we leave it to his particular understanding of religion to show him what that means. We also teach him that his brothers are there to help him. At one point at the beginning of the journey the candidate hears the words, "... arise, follow your guide, and fear not what man can do unto you." We do not leave the candidate to figure it out for himself. We provide him with a guide—a guide upon "whose fidelity he can—with the utmost confidence—rely." In a larger sense, the lodge itself will be his guide. The lodge has a responsibility not only to confer the degrees of Masonry upon him when he is ready at each stage, but to help him understand the inner meaning of what is being taught by that degree. It is this process of helping the candidate that is addressed by a new term in Freemasonry—"Masonic Formation."

Masonic Formation may be described as the systematic assistance the lodge gives to the candidate as he progresses along his Masonic journey. It consists of "candidate education" and of "Masonic education"—but it is much, much more. Properly understood, "Masonic Formation is the matrix into which the teachings of Freemasonry are embedded. Masonic Formation is intertwined with the three degrees of Ancient Craft Masonry, but it goes beyond that to make the teachings of each degree clear, and to help the candidate transform himself by means of what the degree is intended to teach. When our operative brethren built the magnificent cathedrals of old, they built not only walls, but arches and flying buttresses which enabled the building to soar to the heavens. These arches were not built merely by stacking one stone on another as a wall is built. They were built on forms—forms made of wood—around which the stones were arranged until the arch itself was finished and strong enough to hold up the weight of the building for century after century. In a similar fashion, a lodge supports a candidate until he is able to sustain the superstructure of Freemasonry in his own life without the need for additional artificial support of a temporary nature. This process is also called Masonic Formation.

Masonic Formation thus combines two new symbols in Masonry—the concept of "forming" a man into that "house not made with hands, eternal in the heavens," as our ritual puts it. And to it is added the symbol of a journey—a journey that begins before a man even becomes a Mason, and which will continue throughout his lifetime. Freemasonry provides the equipment for this journey by encouraging a Mason to use the teachings of Freemasonry as a guide each day of his life. It also presupposes that the purpose of the journey may be the journey itself. While Freemasons are encouraged to look to their own particular religion for the larger meaning of the end of life, Freemasonry itself concentrates on the road that leads there. Each day can—or should—be enriched by a deeper understanding of the part we play in the progress of humanity, and of our own contribution to this progress.

Masonic Formation is a powerful program. In the pages that follow, you will learn more about what it means, and what it can do for your lodge.

A MEMBER OF IT

By John L. Cooper III
California Freemason, Fall 2006

In the recitation of our ritual, phrases fall from the tongue with the ease of long-practiced familiarity. This very familiarity is what gives comfort to hearing the ritual spoken correctly, and with clarity and feeling. However, this very familiarity can obscure meaning. That is particularly true of the "charge"—the pithy summary of the teachings of each degree given to the candidate as the last—or almost the last—instruction of the occasion. For those listening to those familiar words, the lateness of the hour, and the anticipation of the food and drink to come, may cause them to pay less than normal attention to the words. And yet there is a powerful message in each of these charges—a distillation of important Masonic teachings—which deserves to be pondered.

The charges of the three degrees of Masonry are the membership rules. They are those things which are the indispensable demonstration that a Mason is a member of our ancient and honorable fraternity. With the observance of these rules a man demonstrates to the world at large, and to his brethren, that he is a Mason. Without the observance of these membership rules, he demonstrates the opposite. A dues receipt is evidence that he has paid his annual subscription to his lodge, or holds a lifetime membership therein. But how he lives is his evidence that he is a Mason. What are our membership rules? They are easy to list, when we stop to look carefully at the charges of the three degrees of Masonry. Here is a simple list from the First Degree of Masonry—the "marks of a Mason" by which we will know him to be such:

- He regards the volume of the Sacred Law as the great light in his profession as a Mason. Freemasonry does not specify that volume; only a man's religion can do that. But we expect him to live a life that demonstrates that he holds his particular faith sacred—the emblem of which is the Sacred Law upon which he was obligated as a Mason.

- He will show forth that commitment to the sacred by how he talks and acts. "God," for a Mason, is not an oath uttered in frustration, but the name of the Supreme Being

61

whose love created the world, and who holds all Masons in the hollows of his hands.

- He will act with his neighbor upon the square. In doing so, he will demonstrate a commitment not only to justice, but to mercy; he will do whatever he can to relieve the distress of others just as he would want them to do the same for him.

- He will take care of himself physically, mentally, morally, and spiritually. He will use the talents with which God has blessed him to the glory of God, and for the welfare of others.

- He will be an exemplary citizen. This characteristic comes out not only in loyalty to his country, but by his whole attitude toward the law, which is at the base of peace and good order in society. He isn't a good citizen only when it is convenient. And by never losing sight of the allegiance due to his country, he understands that the burdens of such an allegiance require an active commitment to the daily practice of that citizenship.

- He practices the "domestic and public virtues." In other words, he lives his private life as if the whole world had a window into his soul. He is not a hypocrite. His public image is untarnished, and his private life reflects it perfectly.

- He is faithful to every trust committed to him. He keeps the promises he makes, and especially those solemn promises he entered into when he became a Mason.

Those characteristics of a Mason are all listed in the charge of the Entered Apprentice degree, and similar ones are found in the Fellow Craft degree and Master Mason degree. They are the "marks of membership" in the Masonic fraternity. They are the proof that he is a Mason—far more important than a piece of paper which says that he has contributed financially to his lodge.

Membership in Freemasonry isn't about joining a fraternity; it isn't about being in good standing because one's dues are paid; and it isn't about how long one has been such a member. Membership is the living proof that a Mason exhibits each day to his family, his lodge, his community, and his world, that he is a Mason. The marks of membership are easy to see. They are what really makes a man a Mason.

THE FRATERNITY AND THE FLAG

By John L. Cooper III
California Freemason, Winter 2007

Some of the mystique of Freemasonry is the contrast between seeming opposites, which it successfully harmonizes as a new and more powerful understanding emerges. One such contrast is that a Mason is expected to both be a loyal supporter of his country, while at the same time acknowledging that the brotherhood to which he belongs includes men who owe allegiance to a country other than his own. A Freemason is expected to love his native land, while acknowledging that his "family" includes men of every language, race, culture, and homeland. It was a Freemason who penned these immortal lines:

> Breathes there the man, with soul so dead,
> Who never to himself hath said,
> This is my own, my native land!
> Whose heart hath ne'er within him burn'd,
> As home his footsteps he hath turn'd,
> From wandering on a foreign strand!
> If such there breathe, go, mark him well;
> For him no Minstrel raptures swell;
> High though his titles, proud his name,
> Boundless his wealth as wish can claim;
> Despite those titles, power, and pelf,
> The wretch, concentred all in self,
> Living, shall forfeit fair renown,
> And, doubly dying, shall go down
> To the vile dust, from whence he sprung,
> Unwept, unhonour'd, and unsung.

The author of these lines was Sir Walter Scott, and the lines are from the *Lay of the Last Minstrel*, published in 1805. Scott was a member of St. David Lodge No. 36 on the roll of the Grand Lodge of Scotland. He had become a Master Mason in that lodge on March 2, 1801—just a few years before he wrote these memorable lines. Scott may have had in mind the lessons that Freemasonry taught him about love of country, and then as now, the ritual of Freemasonry clearly states the importance of the linking of family, flag, and country. Listen to what we tell an Entered Apprentice Mason:

As a Citizen you are enjoined to be exemplary in the discharge of your civil duties, by never proposing or countenancing any act which may have a tendency to subvert the peace and good order of society; by paying due obedience to the laws under whose protection you live, and by never losing sight of the allegiance due to your country.

There is no doubt that Freemasonry not only encourages patriotism and a love of one's country, but expects that to be one of the leading characteristics of a Freemason. And yet, Freemasonry is a universal brotherhood, the ties of which reach across national boundaries, and—as the *Constitutions of 1723* state—"...Masonry becomes the Center of Union, and the Means of conciliating true Friendship among Persons that must else have remain'd at a perpetual Distance."

During the Revolutionary War, for example, there were not only Masons on both sides of the conflict, but Masonic lodges as well—military lodges attached to regiments in the American Army and in the British Army. These lodges carried their paraphernalia in "lodge chests," which sometimes were captured by the enemy. We know that there were instances when a truce would be called in the fighting so that the paraphernalia could be returned to the other side. Loyalty to one's country did not undermine a belief on either side that Freemasonry was important enough to stop the war for a moment, and act as brothers on the field of battle.

The Civil War also abounded in stories of brotherhood despite the heated emotions that prevailed amongst the troops on either side. Allen E. Roberts has documented many of these episodes, and one of them is memorialized in the Friend to Friend statue on the battlefield at Gettysburg, erected by the Grand Lodge of Pennsylvania, and pictured elsewhere in this magazine. How does this come about? And how can Masonry be both patriotic, and at the same time universal in its brotherhood?

First, Freemasonry never asks a man to choose between his family and his country and his fraternity. At the core of Freemasonry is a clear and unambiguous commitment to take care of one's family—and a brother's family as well. And that commitment extends to his country as well. Secondly, Freemasonry clearly teaches that all men, whatever their "native land" may be, are entitled to our regard. We learn in the first degree of Masonry that we should "regard the whole human species as one family..."

Lastly, Freemasonry shows that the path of brotherhood can lead us into new ways of understanding—ways that allow us to rise above our own present interest, and place ourselves in the shoes of another. That is what is behind the stories of unexpected acts of charity and kindness toward a man who was otherwise an enemy in time of war. It enabled a Union soldier to render an act of charity and kindness to a Confederate soldier even in the midst of war—because his "enemy" was also his brother. Love of one's country does not preclude loving others who serve a different flag and a different nation. In that sense, Freemasonry is truly universal.

THE HOME OF THE MUSES

By John L. Cooper III
California Freemason, Spring 2007

The term "museum" is commonly used to describe a place where historical and artistic treasures are housed. However, there is a Masonic connection with the word itself, and the lecture of the Fellow Craft degree speaks of the importance of preserving the most important treasures of the past. Let's take a closer look.

The Greek word *mouseion* means a temple to the "muses". The most famous temple to the Muses, from which our current word is derived, was built by Ptolemy II of Egypt in the third century before the Common Era. It was built at Alexandria, Egypt, the city founded by Alexander the Great. Ptolemy I had been one of Alexander's generals, and after Alexander's death, he became Pharaoh of Egypt—founding the Ptolemaic Dynasty, the last of whom was the famous Cleopatra. Around the musaion, or temple of the Muses, a great library was built—the Royal Library of Alexandria. In its time it was one of the greatest intellectual institutions in the world—for it was not only a library, but a great university and teaching institution. Until its destruction at the end of the fourth century, it housed the greatest collection of books the world had ever seen. Its destruction meant the irretrievable loss of much of the learning of the ancient world—books by famous authors whose works are now known only their titles.

This great loss was even more keenly felt during the Renaissance, when Europe once more discovered the learning of the classical world —and mourned the loss to learning that could never be recovered. The impact of this event may well have influenced the wording in the lecture of the Fellow Craft degree, which also speaks of a great loss to the craft. Listen to the words from that lecture:

> The lapse of time, the ruthless hand of ignorance, and the devastations of war, have laid waste and destroyed many valuable monuments of antiquity on which the utmost exertions of human genius were employed. Even the Temple of Solomon, so spacious and magnificent, and constructed by so many celebrated artists, escaped not the unsparing ravages of barbarous force. Freemasonry, notwithstanding, has still survived. The attentive ear receives the sound from the instructive tongue, and the mysteries of Masonry are safely lodged in the repository of faithful breasts. Tools and

implements of architecture most expressive are selected by the Fraternity to imprint upon the memory wise and serious truths; and thus, through the succession of ages, are transmitted unimpaired the most excellent tenets of our Institution.

We commonly interpret this passage as referring to great building of antiquity – an interpretation encouraged by the reference to the Temple of Solomon. However it is equally likely the authors of this passage had in mind the great loss of learning occasions by the destruction of books and artifacts at the end of the classical age – symbolized by the destruction of the Royal Library and Museum at Alexandria. The reference to the mysteries of Freemasonry being safe by being saved by being handed down "mouth to ear" so to speak, tells us that some things are so precious that their protection can only be confided to those who possess the three precious "jewels" of a Fellow Craft Mason: the attentive ear, the instructive tongue and the faithful breast.

Museums and libraries are important to the preservation of treasures of the past. More important is the preservation of the essence of the past when the past itself cannot be recovered. In his science fiction novel *Fahrenheit 451*, Ray Bradbury posits a world in the future in which books are banned. The only way that the great literature of the past can be preserved is by memorizing books. Men and women in his story choose a book to memorize – and they become that "book" – the only transmission possible in a world that has burnt all the books themselves. But the books are not lost, for younger disciples are taught to memorize the books by the older men and women who have already memorized them – handing on to posterity the wisdom of the past. It is an intriguing story. And one with a very Masonic lesson.

Freemasonry has survived because Freemasons have learned the lessons that Freemasonry has to teach. They have made them a part of their lives – they have become living books on Freemasonry. If there ever comes a day when every library, every museum, every historical treasure is destroyed, it would be a great tragedy for humanity. But if there ever comes a time when humanity forgets the teachings of Freemasonry, the tragedy would be even greater. The former loss may be recovered, or at least partly recovered, as we have gradually recovered much of the wisdom of ancient times. But if brotherly love, relief, truth, temperance, fortitude, prudence and justice perish from the earth, our loss is a loss indeed. The greatest museum that Freemasonry has is you. Think about it.

The Springs Gush Forth

By John L. Cooper III
California Freemason, Summer 2007

If you have ever stood on the edge of a mountain stream as it tumbles down to the valley below, you will appreciate the power that seems to be in the rushing water. As a hiker, I have often thus stood and admired the works of our Great Creator as exhibited in the mighty works of nature. Water gathers from many springs and rivulets as it comes down the mountainside, becoming a part of the mountain stream that becomes, in turn, a rushing river. As it twists and turns on its way to the valley floor, it gains in power, and indeed in beauty. Its splashing waters tumble over, under and around the rocks in the riverbed as it makes its way to the placid and calm lake at the foot of the mountain. When last I stood on the verge of such a stream, the words of Psalm 42 came to mind:

> As a deer longs for the flowing
> Streams,
> So my soul longs for you,
> O God.
> Deep calls to deep
> At the thunder of your cataracts;
> All your waves and your billows
> Have all gone over me...

When you and I first became Masons we were asked a very important question: "In whom do you put your trust?" Such a simple question, but what a profound meaning in that question. In those times in life when things seem to go well, it is easy to respond, "In God! My trust is in God!" And, of course, it is – or you and I would not have gone any further in Masonry. But when troubles assail us, when life does not go as we would have planned, when adversity afflicts us, and our trust in God seems sorely tried, it is harder to respond, "In God! My trust is in God!" But that is when the response is needed most. And it is here that the symbolism of the Psalmist speaks to the heart. To see what I mean, read the last half of Psalm 42 first:

> Deep calls to deep
> At the thunder of your cataracts;
> All your waves and your billows

Have all gone over me…

When the misfortunes of life seem to sweep over us, as a mountain stream cascading down the mountainside, when the thunder of the crashing waters and all the waves and billows seem to overwhelm us, when "deep calls to deep" in the words of the poet – then, and only then can we truly understand the meaning of the question, "In whom do you put your trust?" And with the question, comes the answer – symbolically represented by the first stanza of the psalm:

As a deer longs for the flowing
Streams,
So my soul longs for you,
O God.

This stanza speaks of the stream as it comes to the foot of the mountain. Its imagery is that of the stream at rest, a stream calm enough for the deer to drink from, the quiet pools that form on the valley floor. And so it is with our souls. Freemasonry can ask no more of a man than that he make this firm commitment of faith at the beginning of his Masonic journey. And it can offer him no greater reward than the understanding that when he needs it most, he will find the answers he needs beside "the flowing streams."

In whom do you put your trust?

WHO WAS HIRAM ABIFF?

By John L. Cooper III
California Freemason, Fall 2007

Those of you old enough to remember the radio version of *The Lone Ranger* may remember the famous tag line at the end of almost every show: "Who was that masked man?" The question was always asked by someone who had been rescued from dire circumstances by the Lone Ranger — whose identity was kept a closely guarded secret from those he helped.

In a similar way, Masons may ask, "Who was Hiram Abiff?" We know a little about him from our Masonic degrees—but not a lot. In fact, we do not know much more about where he came from and how he got to his position of prominence in Masonry than we know about where the Lone Ranger came from, and how he got to be the famous rescuer of those in trouble on the Western frontier.

The name Hiram first appears in the Bible in the Book of First Kings. In chapter seven we find that:

> Now King Solomon invited and received Hiram from Tyre. He was the son of a widow of the tribe of Naphtali, whose father, a man of Tyre, had been an artisan in bronze; he was full of skill, intelligence, and knowledge in working bronze. He came to King Solomon, and did all his work.

He is not called Hiram Abiff in this passage, and it is only in the Book of Second Chronicles that we learn that his name was Abiff (or something similar to that), and that he was sent to King Solomon by another Hiram— King Hiram of Tyre. Here is what is written in Second Chronicles 2:11–14:

> Then King Hiram of Tyre, answered in a letter that he sent to Solomon, 'I have dispatched Huram-abi, a skilled artisan, endowed with understanding, the son of one of the Danite women, his father a Tyrian. He is trained to work in gold, silver, bronze, iron, stone, and wood, and in purple, blue, and crimson fabrics and fine linen, and to do all sorts of engraving and execute any design that may be assigned to him, with your artisans, the artisans of my lord, your father David.'

From these meager biblical sources, the Masonic legend of Hiram Abiff has been created. There is no mention in the Bible that he was the architect of King Solomon's Temple. That is a Masonic invention. However, he is depicted as a skilled worker in various media—metal, wood, and stone, as well as fabrics. He was also an engraver, and good at artistic designs. It was from these references that he was transformed in our legend to become the architect of the Temple at Jerusalem, "well skilled in arts and sciences." It looks as if we took an ordinary craftsman and made him into something else. Or did we? There is another story here that needs to be told.

Freemasonry teaches by symbol and allegory. The concept of a symbol is easy; the concept of an allegory is more difficult. We can all understand the symbol of the twenty-four inch gauge. That measuring tool, used by stonemasons to measure and lay out their work, represents time—the irreducible minimum of 24 hours which is given to each of us every day. We can have no more, and we have no less. What we do with those 24 hours makes a difference, and Freemasonry helps us to understand why it is important for God, and our family, to get a share of that time, as well as "our usual vocations," and our "refreshment and repose."

The legend of Hiram Abiff is an allegory. It is not about a real human being who was the architect of the Temple, even though the story is based on the real Hiram Abiff found in the Bible. Instead, it is about someone who takes the talents that God has given him, and makes a difference. In our allegory, Hiram Abiff is a man "endowed with understanding" to transform the ordinary into the extraordinary. We depict him as someone who knew how to take common stone and craft it into a magnificent building—perhaps the most magnificent that has ever been built. He is a man "full of skill, intelligence, and knowledge" (the words from the Bible) who could build for eternity. He is a man whose devotion to duty, and to the promises he has made, make him an example worthy of all emulation. We remind the newly raised Master Mason that Hiram Abiff is someone to imitate, and that, therefore, he should never let any motive cause him to swerve from his duty, violate his vows, or betray a trust. If he "gets it," then, like Hiram Abiff, he will be someone who will make a difference.

Hiram Abiff is pictured in our allegory as a man and a Mason who made a difference—not because of what he possessed, but because of what he did with that which he possessed. You can do that, too, with what you possess. You, too, can make a difference—just like Hiram Abiff!

Who was Hiram Abiff?

He was someone who made a difference.

BEGINNING THE MASONIC JOURNEY
The Entered Apprentice Mason

By John L. Cooper III
California Freemason, Winter 2008

Ancient craft Masonry consists of three degrees—and no more: Entered Apprentice Mason, Fellow Craft Mason, and Master Mason. Students of Freemasonry have long known that the second and third degrees evolved from the first one. That makes the Entered Apprentice degree the foundation of ancient craft Masonry and, in some respects, its most important degree.

As stonemasons laid the first stone of a building in a manner that would ensure the stability of the rest of the structure, so Freemasons today confer the degree of Entered Apprentice Mason so that the beginning of a Mason's life is "well formed, true and trusty."

The term "Entered" in "Entered Apprentice Mason" is derived from the custom of officially enrolling an apprentice in the lodge. In operative days this ceremony often took place at age 14, the age at which a young man was entering the threshold of manhood, and could understand the commitments that he was making. Today we have advanced the age to 18, although for many years in California, that age was 21.

Whether the age is 14, 18, or 21, the idea is the same. A young man who is "entered" in the lodge as an Entered Apprentice Mason has been formally accepted by the lodge as a member, and he, in turn, has accepted his responsibility as a Mason. The entire ceremony of "making a Mason," which is an old term for conferring the first degree of Masonry on an Entered Apprentice, is designed to firmly bind the new Mason to Freemasonry. Of great importance at the beginning of his journey as a Mason is the promise he makes. Often misunderstood, the promise to keep the secrets of Freemasonry is really a promise to listen before speaking, to learn before teaching, and to incorporate Freemasonry into one's life before proceeding. I cannot speak about that which I do not yet know, and I cannot write down the things that I do not yet understand. There is a mystery here—and every Entered Apprentice is taught to make this mystery the first step on his journey.

We often think of Entered Apprentice Masons as young men, and in operative days, they were. Today, in our speculative days, an Entered Apprentice may be of any age. As long as he meets the minimum age of 18 and is capable of "understanding the art," he can be made a Mason. Most Entered Apprentice Masons today are mature men in their late 30s or early 40s. Some are younger, and some are older. But all begin their journey in Freemasonry as an Entered Apprentice and are expected to pursue that journey as long as life gives them opportunity. Chronological age is not a factor; mental age is. And at any age we expect an Entered Apprentice to learn what Freemasonry means, and to incorporate its teachings into his life.

Is anyone truly "too old" to become a Mason? Is anyone truly "too young" to understand the mysteries of Masonry? Consider this:

Ted Williams, at age 42, slammed a home run in his last official time at bat.

Mickey Mantle, age 20, hit 23 home runs his first full year in the major leagues.

Golda Meir was 71 when she became prime minister of Israel.

William Pitt II was 24 when he became prime minister of Great Britain.

George Bernard Shaw was 94 when one of his plays was first produced.

Mozart was just 7 when his first composition was published.

Benjamin Franklin was a newspaper columnist at 16 and a framer of the United States Constitution when he was 81.

You are never really too old to become an Entered Apprentice Mason—and never too young. Although we set lower limits for applying for the degrees of Masonry, and our mental vigor sets the upper limits, between these two poles an Entered Apprentice begins his Masonic journey. Whenever you began yours—young or old—you still have time to realize in your life the meaning of becoming an Entered Apprentice Mason. Today is the first day of the rest of your life.

SIR ALEXANDER FLEMING—SCIENTIST AND FREEMASON
His passion for relieving distress led to a moldy discovery

By John L. Cooper III
California Freemason, Spring 2008

It is probable that at some time in your life you visited your doctor for a minor infection and were given a prescription for an antibiotic, which quickly cleared it up before it became a life-threatening condition. You may have filled the prescription and taken the medicine without a thought as to what life would be like for you if no such remedy were available. And yet, before 1928, there were no antibiotics available to control infections, and those who contracted them could expect a serious and life-threatening condition to easily develop. Thanks to a Freemason, we enjoy access to these powerful remedies—a Mason by the name of Alexander Fleming.

Sir Alexander Fleming (1881–1955) was a Scottish biologist who was awarded the Nobel Prize in Medicine in 1945 for the discovery of penicillin. That date is important because that was when World War II ended. It is reliably estimated that up to 15% of the wounded in that epic conflict survived as a result of the discovery of penicillin.

Fleming served in World War I as a captain in the British Army Medical Corps, and saw firsthand the deaths which resulted from battle wounds. In those days the only treatment was the application of simple antiseptics to the outside of wounds. Fleming noted that these antiseptics often caused more of a problem than they cured by destroying the body's natural defenses. Bacteria deep in the wounds could not be attacked by these antiseptics, and surface treatment destroyed the body's own antibiotic, lysozyme. In 1928 he discovered, quite by accident, that bacteria were destroyed by penicillin mold growing in a petri dish. His personal experience in World War I, and his continuing interest in ways to control infection, caused him to realize the potential of this simple mold as an antibiotic agent—and to begin his experiments which led to the production of this life-saving drug.

Great men in history are often the subjects of legends, so it should be no surprise that there are two legends associated with Sir Alexander Fleming. The first one is that young Winston Churchill's life was saved by Sir Alexander's father, and the second one is that the famous prime minister's life was saved during World War II by Sir Alexander's discovery of penicillin. Neither tale is true, however intriguing they may be.

Truth is much stranger than fiction, and the true story of the discovery of penicillin is one of the great stories of our time. If Fleming had not transformed his experiences as a soldier in World War I into a passion

75

for relieving the distressed, he might never have noticed the moldy petri dish and its implications. And had he not done so, countless lives would have been lost over the years since his amazing discovery. In the Entered Apprentice degree we are taught that our responsibilities to our neighbor go beyond just being a friend. As the ritual tells it, a Mason is to apply what he learns as a Mason to his neighbor by "relieving his distresses and soothing his afflictions ..." Bro. Fleming certainly did that in a big way— and humanity has benefitted by the passion for the conquest of infection that characterized this famous Freemason.

Sir Alexander Fleming was a member of several English lodges and master of two: Santa Maria Lodge No. 2682 in 1925 and Misericordia Lodge 3286 in 1935. In 1942 he served as senior grand deacon of the United Grand Lodge of England and was promoted to the rank of past grand warden in 1948.

Exploring Important Issues in Freemasonry
The California Masonic Symposium

By John L. Cooper III
California Freemason, Summer 2008

Master Masons are told at a critical moment in the third degree that the search for further light in Masonry should be a distinguishing characteristic of all Masons. The California Masonic Symposium provides a place each year for Masons to experience the cutting edge of "Masonic light" in the form of contemporary scholarship.

It also has offered young Masonic scholars a place to speak. In 2007, two prominent young men—one a Mason and one not yet a Mason—presented papers on the impact of Freemasonry in Mexico and its cultural and political history. Both papers were very well received, and symposium participants learned something about Freemasonry "south of the border" that they could never have experienced in any other forum.

The annual symposium began in 2001 as a means of bringing prominent Masonic scholars and speakers to California. Seven symposiums have been held, with a truly impressive list of prominent Masons and Masonic scholars who have participated. A partial list of the scholars who have shared their expertise and knowledge includes:

Rex Hutchens—author of *A Bridge to Light*, and other books. He was the first person to deliver the coveted Henry Wilson Coil Masonic Lecture—a feature of each symposium since 2001.

S. Brent Morris—who wrote *The Complete Idiot's Guide to Freemasonry*—a best-seller—and many other well-known Masonic books.

Dr. Margaret Jacob—perhaps the best-known academic historian of Freemasonry alive today. She has authored several books on Masonry including *Living the Enlightenment: Freemasonry and the Politics of 18th Century Europe*.

Robert L. D. Cooper—Librarian of the Grand Lodge of Scotland, and world-famous speaker on Freemasonry. His lecture on Rosslyn Chapel brought out a crowd of almost 150 participants at Stanford University.

Robert Davis—General secretary of the Scottish Rite at Guthrie, Oklahoma, who spoke on *Freemasonry and the American Indian* in 2004 in San Diego. He will be the featured speaker again in August 2008, on the impact of fraternalism on men in American society. He is the author of *Understanding Manhood in America: Freemasonry's Enduring Path to the Mature Masculine.*

Dr. Gary Leazer—prominent religious scholar and Freemason.

Leon Zeldis—former grand commander of the Supreme Council of the Scottish Rite for the State of Israel.

Dr. Paul Rich—professor of international relations at the University of Puebla, Mexico, and a fellow of the Hoover Institution at Stanford University.

The California Masonic Symposium is designed not only to showcase prominent Masonic scholars, but also to provide a forum for the exploration of ideas important to Freemasons today. In 2003, the symposium at UCLA looked at Freemasonry and the Enlightenment—the eighteenth century cradle of social and political freedom to which the United States is so deeply indebted. That particular symposium also saw prominent scholars from France share the stage with well-known American scholars—and an opportunity for understanding the impact of Freemasonry on modern history.

The California Masonic Symposium has won wide acclaim for the breadth of its topics, and for the depth of its exploration of important issues in Freemasonry today. It is—in the words of the lecture of the third degree—"well calculated to increase knowledge and promote virtue."

The Home of the First Grand Lodge

By John L. Cooper III
California Freemason, Fall 2008

The first grand lodge of Masons in the world was organized in London on June 24, 1717, in the Goose and Gridiron Tavern. It was formed by four "time immemorial" lodges—lodges whose origins are lost in the mists of time.

The Goose and Gridiron tavern was the meeting place of what later became known as the Lodge of Antiquity, and in these borrowed premises the first Grand Lodge was formed. It wasn't until 1776 that Grand Lodge built its first home—at a site which is still the location of the headquarters of the United Grand Lodge of England.

At the quarterly communication of Grand Lodge in October 1768, a proposal was introduced to raise funds to build a home for Grand Lodge. The funds came primarily from fees paid by newly chartered lodges and fees paid to Grand Lodge for registering new members of the constituent lodges.

Sufficient funds had been raised by November 1774 so that the Committee of Charity—virtually the governing board of Grand Lodge—was able to purchase property on Great Queen Street at a cost of £3,150. But in order to fund the enterprise even more quickly, Grand Lodge came up with a new idea in February 1775. Individual Masons were asked to lend £25 to Grand Lodge for the purpose of building the new hall, for which they were granted the right to wear a special medal in recognition. In addition, they were granted the right as individuals to vote at Grand Lodge. Up to this point, only the masters and wardens were permitted to represent their lodges and to vote. When Grand Lodge was in a position to repay the loan to those subscribing, these special voting rights disappeared.

On May 1, 1775, the foundation stone for the building was laid, and on May 23, 1776, the new building was opened and dedicated by the grand master to "Masonry, virtue, universal charity, and benevolence."

Those words have come down to us today as a part of the ceremony performed by Grand Lodge called the "Dedication of Masonic Halls." As charity and benevolence are synonyms for the same concept, our present-day ceremony has shortened the formula used by the Grand Lodge of England in 1776. Today, the grand master dedicates a Masonic hall "... to Freemasonry, virtue, and universal benevolence."

It is easy to remember the year the first Grand Lodge building was

79

dedicated because it is the date of our own Declaration of Independence. It also reminds us that Masons build spiritual as well as physical buildings.

Just as Masonic buildings since 1776 have been dedicated to virtue and universal benevolence, so, too, should our spiritual buildings be dedicated.

IT'S REALLY ABOUT BROTHERHOOD

By John L. Cooper III
California Freemason, October - November 2008

The theme of this issue is "Meeting the Expectations and Needs of Today's New Member." As a Mason from the "older generation," I have often pondered what motivates a young man today to seek out Freemasonry. Many of us are conversant with generational theory— the idea that different generations of men seek different ways to fulfill their expectations of life —and have noted that organizations that do not change to meet those expectations are doomed to extinction. That certainly seemed to be the case in Freemasonry, before the recent surge of interest that is causing a minor flood of applicants in their 20s and 30s. And while many of us from the older generation are very glad that these young men have discovered the institution we treasure and revere, we also wonder whether these new Masons will find what they are looking for in Freemasonry as it exists today in most lodges. In earlier generations, if new Masons didn't find what they wanted, it somehow didn't seem to matter. The prestige of belonging to an organization with the reputation of Masonry was enough for them to keep paying the rather low dues year after year – with never a thought about actually showing up at lodge. We worry that this won't be the case in the future unless Masonry offers them something in the lodge itself.

The new generation of Masons may be different from previous generations in more ways than one. We know that younger Masons are interested in the philosophy, history, ritual, and traditions of Freemasonry. We also know that they care about how they spend their time, and are willing to pay higher dues to enjoy a first-rate fraternal experience. And we know that they have not abandoned a concern for outreach and community service, because lodges that are successful in attracting these younger Masons are also usually at the top of the list for community service as a lodge and for individual giving through organized charities. In addition, we know that they care about taking Masonry out into the world and living it daily. But is there more? I think so. And the words of a young Mason from Washington, D.C., say it better than I can.

In an interview on May 5, 2007 with National Public Radio, David Johnson, the 36-year-old junior warden of Naval Lodge No. 4 under the Grand Lodge of the District of Columbia, was asked what was so attractive about Freemasonry to a young man of his generation. Here is an excerpt reflecting his answer:

... But for many new, younger members, Masonry's attraction lies less in historical icons and artifacts than in its sense of fraternity. Johnson, the junior warden of Naval Lodge 4, says what bonds Masons together is oral tradition: passing knowledge, experience and wisdom from generation to generation. 'It takes another brother to show you the way and take you down the path to get to the enlightenment that we offer,' he says.

I think Bro. Johnson has it right. There is a tremendous attraction to Freemasonry for its mysterious past, its ancient symbols, and the heroic men associated with it. But that isn't enough. It's really about brotherhood. That's why this generation of Masons is interested in being in lodge and with other Masons. You can't get it from books, and you can't get it from television. You can only get it from another Mason.

As Johnson puts it so well, "It takes another brother to show you the way."

The Lodge At Refreshment

By John L. Cooper III
California Freemason, December – January 2009

A Masonic lodge has many curious customs handed down through the years, and none perhaps more curious than the concept of the lodge "at refreshment." In this issue devoted to food and our craft, it seems appropriate to look at the history of the idea of a lodge at refreshment—and the similarly curious idea of a lodge officer whose primary duty is to make sure that Masons don't eat and drink too much!

When the junior warden of a lodge is installed, this is the charge given to him by the installing officer:

> To you is committed the superintendence of the Craft during the hours of refreshment; it is necessary therefore, that you should practice moderation and discretion in the indulgence of your own inclinations, and that you carefully observe that the means of refreshment are not converted to improper or excessive use.

When lodges are at refreshment, and thereby called from Masonic labor, they are under the supervision and control of the junior warden as symbolized in the lodge room by the column on his pedestal. When the lodge is at refreshment, and under his supervision, his column is in the upright position. When it is so positioned, the members are visually reminded that the lodge is at refreshment and that they should pay attention to the junior warden's important role in regulating their conduct.

The origin of this peculiar custom—an officer assigned to make sure that Masons do not eat and drink too much—lies in the early history of our lodges in the 17th and 18th centuries. In those days lodges met in taverns, where food and drink were the primary business of the establishment. They often used a private dining room as their meeting place and met around a horseshoe-shaped table arrangement. The degrees were usually conferred in the space in the middle of the room, with the tables on three sides. Members and officers sat around the outside edge of the tables so that they had a clear view of the ceremonies in the center of the room as well as a clear view of each other, arranged around the table. Unlike our modern customs, they did not confer the degrees in a lodge room and then retire to a separate room for food and drink. They ate and drank in the same lodge room – but only while the lodge was at refreshment and under the control of the junior warden. They were not supposed to carry on with eating and drinking while the degrees were in progress on the floor in front of them.

Then, as now, Masons enjoyed their food and drink. Lodge minute books from those times are filled with bills paid for food, wine, and "punch:" rum punch, which had quite a kick to it. There are still in existence Masonic punchbowls – ceramic bowls highly decorated with Masonic symbols and emblems – which were used by lodges to serve up the punch to members. The service of this food and drink was the responsibility of the stewards; some lodges had more than the customary senior and junior stewards if their membership was large enough to warrant it.

It is also clear that Masons of those days did not always use good judgment about how much to eat and drink. It is probably from this era that our first Masonic cardinal virtue, temperance, comes. In the language of our ritual, "Temperance is that due restraint upon the affections and passions which renders the body tame and governable, and frees the mind from the allurements of vice. This virtue should be your constant practice, as you are thereby taught to avoid excess ..."

While Masons today are unlikely to be tempted to return to the riotous behavior of earlier times, there is still the danger that we will forget the importance of temperance as a cardinal virtue. Too much of a good thing is hazardous to anyone's health, whether that applies to food and drink or to getting carried away with too much fun at someone else's expense. We still install a junior warden in each lodge to remind us that too much food, drink, or "fun" can be ruinous to our health – and to the health of the lodge. Each one of us should take it as our personal duty to see "that the means of refreshment are not converted to improper or excessive use."

No More Than He Really May Deserve
Helping our youth orders the right way

By John L. Cooper III

California Freemason, February – March 2009

In 1723, Dr. James Anderson laid a new version of the Ancient Charges before the Grand Lodge in London. Before the formation of the first grand lodge in 1717, lodges read from copies of the Ancient Charges at the making of a Mason. Realizing that a contemporary version was required for the reorganized state of Freemasonry under the new grand lodge, Dr. Anderson created the foundation document of modern Freemasonry. The section of this work called "The Charges of a Free-Mason" was divided into six parts, and contained an interesting mix of old and new. Some of the material obviously referred to Freemasonry as a stonemasons' guild, while other material reflected the contemporary state of Freemasonry as a purely philosophical society.

In Charge V, "Of the Management of the Craft in Working," Anderson set forth the rules for working Masons. Here, he said that "The Master, knowing himself to be able of Cunning, shall undertake the Lord's Work as reasonably as possible, and truly dispend his Goods as if they were his own; nor to give more Wages to any Brother or Apprentice than he really may deserve."

At first, this seems to be language from the operative days of the craft, referring to actual working stonemasons. But is it? Freemasonry's teachings are full of surprises, and sometimes, what seems to have an obvious meaning has a symbolic meaning, as well. I believe that this excerpt from the Constitution of 1723 has just such a symbolic meaning, and that it applies to our Masonic youth as well as to Masons.

In this issue of the *California Freemason* magazine, you will learn much about our Masonic youth orders and the adults who work with them. It might seem strange to suggest that an important principle in working with our youth is not to give them more than they "really may deserve," to quote the Charges of a Free-Mason of 1723. But it was an important principle in the days of operative Masonry, and it is an important principle today. To give someone more than he may deserve is to take away the privilege of earning something. The Entered Apprentice who was paid for work that he did not do learned nothing about the value of the work, just as giving our Masonic youth something without teaching them the value of working to obtain it teaches them nothing about the pride of accomplishment that comes from hard work.

I am not speaking of giving our youth places to meet at prices that they can afford. All too many lodges fail to make their facilities available to the youth orders at an affordable rental rate. Nor am I suggesting that lodges not support our youth orders financially; Our youth orders need our financial support in order to thrive. But we should not give our youth orders the wrong kind of support, by doing things for them that they can do for themselves.

An important principle in all three of our Masonic youth orders is that they are a learning experience for leadership—and learning to be a leader involves making mistakes. As adult leaders of our Masonic youth orders, we are there to serve as a "safety net," but we are not there to do the job for them. If youths plan and carry out a community or Masonic service event on their own, they learn how to do it. If they plan and conduct meetings, they learn how to make meetings an attractive and productive experience. And if we involve them in a meaningful way in some of our adult community service activities, they learn not only what adults do, but values of those adults that they can admire and copy.

Supporting our youth orders is much more than buying a car wash ticket or paying them to serve dinner. It must involve a personal commitment to working with them, and a personal commitment to not do the job for them. As in operative days, giving someone "more Wages... than he really may deserve" is not helping at all. But giving our youth orders what they really deserve—the chance to achieve something of merit—is helping them the right way. Whether it is a "perfect ashlar," as in the days of the working stonemasons, or the perfect community service project today, we give our young people what they truly deserve if we let them do it themselves – with our guidance, encouragement, and support.

Dr. Anderson summarized all this in a later paragraph in Charge V: "None shall discover Envy at the Prosperity of a Brother, nor supplant him or put him out of his Work, if he be capable to finish the same..."

The Beehive and Community Service

By John L. Cooper III
California Freemason, April – May 2009

The beehive is an emblem of industry, and recommends the practice of that virtue to all created beings, from the highest seraph in heaven to the lowest reptile of the dust. It teaches us that as we came into the world rational and intelligent beings, so we should ever be industrious ones; never sitting down contented while our fellow-creatures around us are in want ...

Many Masons in California rarely hear about the symbol of the beehive. This excerpt from the third degree lecture is optional, and has been since the 1920s. Past Grand Master Frederick L. Sorsabal made the beehive an important emblem during his term of office, and thus called it into focus. This often neglected and unknown symbol is very much worth our attention.

The ritual of Freemasonry offers thoughts on our symbols, but these thoughts are not intended to be comprehensive. Nor is the explanation of a symbol in the ritual meant to be exhaustive. It is intended to point us to further study of the symbol—a study that can take a lifetime of contemplation and devotion. So it is with the beehive. The insight offered in the ritual for the beehive is only one aspect of this symbol—and perhaps not even the most important one.

There is another interpretation of the beehive that should be called to our attention besides that of an industrious worker. That has to do with the communal nature of the work of the hive, and especially the work within the larger community in which it is located. If we were to place a beehive within a closed room, with no outlet to the world at large, the bees would die. Even if the room was very large, and the bees were allowed to exit and enter the hive freely, the hive would die. To survive, the beehive must be able to work in the world at large.

Bees obtain sugars from flowers, which they bring back to the hive to transform into the honey which feeds them. In doing so, they move pollen from one flower to another, allowing the flowers to reproduce and live. This beneficial and symbiotic relationship is well-known. Without it certain flowers would die; without it the hive would die. It is not a choice of either/or—it is a question of both.

Not all bees go forth from the hive to do this work. The queen remains behind because she has other important duties to perform. But as a whole, the hive must work in the outside world in order to live.

In certain times and in certain places, Masons have missed this important lesson. They have concentrated on the work done inside the lodge, with little thought of the community in which they live. The lodge becomes their sole interest as individuals, and the lodge fails to connect to the community. In time, that lodge will die, much as the beehive will die if the bees cannot – or do not—go out into the world where their true work is performed.

As with the beehive, we recognize that not all members can work in the community at large. Age and infirmity will keep some from doing what others must do on their behalf. But as Masons we must work and do Masonry outside the lodge, too—or the lodge will die.

The hive thrives when bees do their valued and valuable work for others. The lodge thrives when Masons do their valued and valuable work for others. We can never "sit down contented," as the ritual puts it, when there is work to do in the community. And a good thing it is, for such would be the death of our lodge.

Freemasonry will thrive when we remember the hive!

THE THREE SOURCES OF OUR COUNTRY'S GREATNESS

By John L. Cooper III
California Freemason, June-July 2009

DeMolay International, one of our three Masonic youth orders, makes a powerful statement of our fraternity's commitment to this country's public schools, in word, in symbol, and in deed. Those who attend a DeMolay ceremony cannot miss the stack of books placed on the altar next to the open Bible, our country's flag hanging nearby. In the public installation ceremony, the installing officer places these books on the altar, stating that they are "a symbol of the intellectual liberty, without which there could be neither civil nor religious freedom." He goes on to say, "They are particularly emblematic of the great public school system of our country, the foundation of that universal enlightenment which is the crowning glory of our institutions."

The installing officer then reminds us that:

> Devoted championship of our public schools is a cardinal teaching of the Order of DeMolay. We are unalterably opposed to the same building housing a school, a church, and a seat of civil government. Civil, religious and intellectual liberty are the three sources of our country's greatness, but they must stand alone, upon separate foundations and under separate roofs.

Just as we treasure our civil and religious liberties in this free land, so must we treasure our intellectual liberties, represented by our public schools. For the sake of intellectual liberty, our public schools today sustain challenges such as never before.

Inside the base of the Statue of Liberty are inscribed these famous lines from a poem by Emma Lazarus:

> Give me your tired, your poor,
> Your huddled masses yearning to breathe free...

Through the centuries, men and women have fled to our shores to realize this promise of freedom, which extends to the public education system. As a result, our public schools must accommodate dozens of languages spoken by children whose parents came to this land to "breathe free," as the poem says. Our public schools bring together children from varied social and economic backgrounds, and can become an unintentional battleground for culture wars.

Great institutions will always be subject to criticism, and as a result of these challenges, criticism often seems to swamp our public schools. It blinds us to their primary purpose, which they have nobly achieved: fostering "that intellectual liberty, without which there could be neither civil nor religious freedom."

Parents, of course, are not required to send their children to our public schools. They may choose private schools, religiously based schools, or even to school their children at home, as long as they meet certain minimal standards. But such freedom of choice, however valued, does not and cannot take away the great achievement of our public schools.

Public schools are much more than just a public alternative to private institutions. They set the standard for all the other forms of education—and not the other way around. As the DeMolay ritual puts it, they are "the foundation of that universal enlightenment which is the crowning glory of our institutions."

Universal enlightenment is at the heart of the mission of Freemasonry—a mission devoted to the pursuit of knowledge and the ability to use it wisely. In a real sense, our public schools are a realization of that Masonic ideal. It cannot be better expressed than in these words, from the ritual of DeMolay International:

> We, therefore, place these books upon the Altar and I solemnly enjoin the members of this Chapter ever to stand unswervingly for the protection and perpetuity of the free public schools, the citadel of our safety and the source of the only real freedom possible in a government of the people, by the people and for the people.

Past Perfect

By John L. Cooper III
California Freemason, August – September 2009

This issue of *California Freemason* shows that we have a lot of Masonic heritage worth preserving – much more than one might realize in an era when lodges frequently sell off historic buildings to seek new homes or consolidate. It is perhaps easy to forget that Freemasonry has been preserving its heritage in other ways, for longer than any of our buildings have stood – through ritual.

The ritual of Freemasonry is filled with allusions to the past. In the first degree, the Entered Apprentice is told that he should "Be faithful to the trust committed to your care, and manifest your fidelity to your principles... by adhering to the Ancient Landmarks thereof."

As a Fellow Craft, he is admonished to "preserve the ancient usages and customs of the Fraternity sacred and inviolate; and thus, by your example, induce others also to hold them in due veneration."

As a Master Mason, he is reminded once more of the importance of preserving this heritage: "Our Ancient Landmarks you are carefully to preserve, and never to suffer them, on any pretense, to be infringed; and you are never to countenance any deviation from our established customs." By this time, the new Master Mason should be very much aware of the importance Freemasonry attaches to preserving our heritage—at least, the heritage of our core teachings, expressed through ritual.

And yet, the words and customs used to demonstrate core teachings has changed over the years. What was once a simple ceremony of admission in the seventeenth century has evolved into a ritual of three degrees, accompanied by lectures which we know were written at a much later date than the degrees themselves. Masons once met in inns and taverns, using makeshift lodge rooms with minimal furnishings and visible expressions of Masonic symbols. So temporary were the visuals used with the degrees that they were often marked in chalk, charcoal, and clay on the floor of the meeting room and washed out afterward with a bucket and mop.

Nor have we uniformly preserved other customs, which our Masonic ancestors once thought all-important. Masons in the eighteenth century wore white gloves in lodge, and attached such importance to the custom that they presented a new Entered Apprentice Mason with his own pair to wear in the lodge and a second pair to give to his lady, a reminder that his life had changed by becoming a Mason. Although some earnestly seek to revive it, that old custom has become obsolete in California.

If this kind of change has occurred, then our commitment to preserving our heritage must be of a different nature. It is. The kind of heritage that has never become obsolete, and never will, is found in the charges—those brief summaries of Masonic teaching, which are the culmination of each degree.

> As a Mason, you are to regard the volume of the Sacred Law as the great light in your profession.... In it, you will learn the important duties which you owe to God, your neighbor, and yourself.

> It is unnecessary to recapitulate the duties which, as a Fellow Craft, you are bound to discharge. Your general good reputation affords satisfactory assurance that you will not suffer any consideration to induce you to act in a manner unworthy of the respectable character which you now sustain.

> Your honor and reputation are concerned in supporting with dignity the respectable character which you now bear. Let no motive, therefore, make you swerve from your duty, violate your vows or betray your trust....

In other words, the heritage that we, as Masons, are expected to preserve is much more than bricks and mortar. It is even more than old lodge customs, no matter how valuable those may be. The most important heritage that Masons are expected to preserve is that which neither "moth and rust doth corrupt, and where thieves [neither] break through and steal" (Matt. 6:19, New American Standard Bible).

Our real heritage is in the mysteries of Masonry—those mysteries "safely lodged in the repository of faithful breasts."

We will go on preserving that heritage for as long as time will last.

WHY BLUE?

By John L. Cooper III
California Freemason, October – November 2009

One of the mysteries of Masonry is the term we have for our lodges. They are called "blue" lodges—but why?

It seems this question should be easily answered, but that is not the case. Standard Masonic encyclopedias and dictionaries will yield a variety of fanciful explanations, many of which are more speculation than fact. However, Masonic references from the early eighteenth century include the use of the color blue, and one such reference in Samuel Prichard's *Masonry Dissected* (1730) may, in fact, be the source of the use of "blue" for our lodges today. Here is the story.

In the eighteenth century, Freemasons were fond of developing Masonic test questions to screen brethren who showed up as visitors to their lodges. The Masonic catechisms of the period—questions and answers used to instruct candidates in the teachings of Freemasonry— occasionally included "catch" questions that would only make sense to someone familiar with the lodge setting. One test question concerned the "gold jacket and blue breeches." Prichard reports this curious dialogue:

Q. Have you seen your Master to-day?
A. Yes.
Q. How was he Cloathed?
A. In a Yellow Jacket and Blue Pair of Breeches.
(*The Yellow Jacket is the Compasses, and the Blue Breeches the Steel Points.*)

Today the compass (or Compasses, as it was spelled in the eighteenth century) is usually made entirely of silver or gold. But originally, the body of the compass was brass – hence the color yellow – and the points were tempered steel – hence the color blue. The test question would clearly be understood by anyone who attended lodge and saw the square and compass resting on the Volume of the Sacred Law.

We know that this symbolism was extended to the actual clothing worn by the master of a lodge on at least one instance. On St. John's Day in June 1725, the Earl of Ross was installed as grand master of the Grand Lodge of Ireland, and was escorted to the place of installation by six lodges. The master of one of these lodges is reported to have worn a "Yellow Jacket and Blue Breeches." This may have been a whimsical reference to the dialogue later reported in *Masonry Dissected*, between those who were "in the know" regarding why the Master was so dressed.

In the lecture of the Entered Apprentice degree, there is a reference to the Holy Bible and square and compass that may be an echo of this eighteenth century esoteric symbolism, now largely lost to us. We learn that:

> The Holy Bible is dedicated to God, it being His inestimable gift to man as the rule and guide of his faith; the Square to the Master, because it is the proper Masonic emblem of his office; and the Compass to the Craft, for by due attention to its use, we are taught to circumscribe our desires and keep our passions within due bounds toward all mankind.

This passage assigns the meaning of the compass to Freemasonry itself, and explains its purpose. As the compass is used to draw circles, so Freemasonry teaches its members to draw a boundary around their conduct so that they do not trespass on the person or feelings of another through unwarranted intrusion of their own particular sectarian beliefs on social, political, and religious matters. The compass becomes a symbol of restraint upon our own passionate beliefs and a concomitant respect for the opinions and beliefs of others.

It is thought by some that the association of the blue of the points of the compass was transferred to Freemasonry as a whole, and especially to the foundational degrees of Freemasonry—the three degrees of ancient craft Masonry: the Entered Apprentice, Fellow Craft, and Master Mason degrees.

Long after our ancestors developed this association, we forgot its origin, and why we now call our lodges "blue" lodges. But this designation may well hark back to the old test question based on a symbolism now lost —the steel points of the compass in the eighteenth century.

The source of the symbolism has been forgotten, but not the continuing meaning behind it. Our blue lodges are still places where we learn the importance of constraining our passions, and practicing a respect for the religious and political opinions of others.

THE TEMPLAR CONNECTION
The hoax behind one of Masonry's most popular myths

By John L. Cooper
California Freemason, December – January 2010

Everyone loves a good story, and the Templar connection with Freemasonry is a good story – even if it is just that – a story, with no historical foundation.

Books such as John Robinson's *Born in Blood* suggested that Freemasonry is really the Medieval Order of Knights Templar in disguise. According to that story, the Knights Templar joined stonemasons lodges in Scotland after the order had been suppressed in 1307, and eventually took over these lodges. As the story goes, the Templars thus survived underground until they emerged into public light with the creation of the first grand lodge in England in 1717.

It makes an interesting tale, but there is no real evidence to support the idea. However, the real story of how Freemasonry came to be associated with the Templars is even more interesting. And this one is true.

Whatever the origin of Freemasonry in England and Scotland (and there are many theories besides that of the fanciful Templar connection), we know that four lodges in London formed the first grand lodge in 1717. Over the next few years, other lodges either joined the new grand lodge, or received charters from it to form new lodges.

It was not long before Freemasonry spread to the continent of Europe, including France and Germany. When it spread to the continent, the simple structure of three degrees that we know as "Ancient Craft Masonry" became embellished with many additional degrees, some of which were subsequently organized into "rites" of one type or another.

Many of these additional degrees added new stories and legends to Freemasonry, one of which was the idea that Freemasonry had originated with the Crusades when knights brought back some form of secret knowledge from the Holy Land. One of the earliest degrees to offer this explanation of Freemasonry was that of the "Scots Master" degree. According to the legend that formed the substance of the degree, knights from Scotland found a great secret buried in a vault in Jerusalem, and brought it back with them to Scotland.

At this stage of development there was no suggestion that these knights were Knights Templar. That had to await a further addition to the story.

The popularity of Freemasonry in France and Germany in the last half of the eighteenth century was enormous. The additional rites and degrees were especially of interest to the wealthy aristocracy in those two countries, and the idea that Freemasonry had its roots in the chivalric class of noble warriors in the Middle Ages held much greater attraction for them than the idea that Freemasons grew out of guilds of stonemasons. It was natural that they would prefer to belong to an organization with an aristocratic heritage rather than one that came from a working class background, and so these upper class Masons seized upon the story of a chivalric origin for Freemasonry with great passion.

One such Mason was Baron von Hund in Germany. Karl Gotthelf, Baron von Hund und Alten-Grotkau, to give him his proper name, was born in 1722. In 1742 he became a Mason at Frankfurt, and the next year traveled to Paris, where he became the senior warden of a lodge at Versailles.

In order to understand what happened next, we have to go back a bit into English history. In 1685 Charles II of England died, and his younger brother, James, came to the throne. A convert to the Roman Catholic faith, he appointed Catholic friends to high positions. In short order civil war broke out over this issue, and James fled to France.

James, however, did not give up. He settled in France, and tried to regain his throne through conspiracy and intrigue. His son continued the effort, and then his grandson, Charles, who was also known as "Bonnie Prince Charlie."

While von Hund was in Paris, he was contacted by someone that he believed to be Bonnie Prince Charlie, but who had disguised himself as the "Knight of the Red Feather."

To this day we don't know if von Hund was actually contacted by Prince Charlie himself in order to sign him up as a supporter (along with his considerable fortune), or whether this was a hoax perpetrated by someone who had no connection to Charles. In any event, this Knight of the Red Feather told von Hund that he was the grand master of the Order of Knights Templar, and showed von Hund a list of grand masters that supposedly had hidden themselves from the authorities for hundreds of years since the death of DeMolay in 1314. He was also told that the Knights Templar had escaped to Scotland and helped Robert the Bruce win the Battle of Bannockburn in 1314, and from that date forward had remained as close allies of the kings of Scotland (and Charles maintained that he was the true king of Scotland).

Von Hund was also apparently told that the Knights Templar had secretly joined lodges of stonemasons in Scotland so that they could remain in hiding for centuries, and that Freemasons were actually the surviving Knights Templar.

Von Hund gullibly swallowed this story, and returned to Germany, eager to share his new knowledge with his fellow Freemasons. All this was in 1742 – four years before the disastrous defeat of Bonnie Prince Charlie at the Battle of Culloden Moor in 1746. If he was behind the attempt to recruit von Hund to the cause, any such efforts collapsed after the battle, for von Hund never again heard from the Knight of the Red Feather. But to his dying day, von Hund believed that the person he had met as the "Knight of the Red Feather" was Charles III of England, Scotland, and Ireland, and that the Freemasons were the descendants of the Knights Templar.

The Masonic rite that is associated with von Hund is the Rite of Strict Observance. He did not found the organization, but became its most prominent member, and it was through this rite that he propagated his "secret knowledge" that Freemasons were actually the surviving Knights Templar. The name "Strict Observance" came from the fact that Masons who belonged to this rite had to swear allegiance to "unknown superiors" —presumably the secret leaders of the Templars that had purportedly contacted von Hund in Paris.

To the basic three degrees of Masonry that we know of today, von Hund added four: Scottish Master, Novice, Templar, and Professed Knight. And the new Rite of Strict Observance took off like a rocket!

Within a few years the Rite of Strict Observance had become so popular that almost all other Masonic rites and degrees in Germany were pushed out. Gone were the simple degrees known to Freemasons the world over as "Ancient Craft Masonry." The Rite of Strict Observance replaced these simple degrees with high-sounding titles and pageantry to which Masons flocked. There is no doubt, also, that they were intrigued with the idea that they were the descendants of the Knight Templar of old. After all, these knights were the cream of the aristocracy in their day, enormously wealthy, and very powerful. How nice to belong to an organization which shared that heritage!

But just as the Rite of Strict Observance quickly rose to prominence, it quickly subsided into obscurity. Torn apart by quarrels amongst its leaders, it did not survive the death of von Hund in 1776—at least, it did not survive as the large and popular Masonic rite it had been.

That same year, the "Young Pretender," Bonnie Prince Charlie, was finally asked if he was the founder of the rite, and he denied any knowledge of it. By this time it was evident that von Hund had been taken in by charlatans, and that all the claims of his rite were bogus. Only his death in 1776 saved him from disgrace.

And that's how the "Templar Legend" entered Freemasonry. We still have Templar degrees in Freemasonry—the 30th degree of the Scottish Rite is one such degree, and the Order of the Temple is another, as well as the Order of DeMolay. However, none of these degrees and orders make the outlandish claim that Baron von Hund made about the secret survival of the Templars and their association with Freemasonry. They celebrate one aspect or another of the chivalry of the Middle Ages, or tell the story of Jacques DeMolay.

So if someone today tells you that Freemasonry is descended from the Knight Templar of old, you now know the real story. The real story is also an interesting tale!

Of the Civil Magistrate, Supreme and Subordinate

By John L. Cooper III
California Freemason, February – March 2010

When George Washington was only two years old, the first Masonic book published in America came off the press of a young printer in Philadelphia named Benjamin Franklin, himself just 26 years old at the time. The book he printed was *The Constitutions of the Free-Masons*, a book that had originally been published in 1723, only eleven years earlier, by the Grand Lodge of England.

One of the most important documents in the history of Freemasonry, these "Constitutions" were the foundation of modern speculative Freemasonry.

A year after Franklin printed *The Constitutions of the Free-Masons* he himself sought membership in the fraternity, and not long after, was provincial grand master of Pennsylvania. The book was widely available to Freemasons in North America, and it is likely that another young Mason, George Washington, was familiar with the contents of this important work after he became an Entered Apprentice Mason in Fredericksburg Lodge, Virginia, in November 1752. It is very likely that he had heard "The Charges of a Free-Mason" from this book read many times, because in those days it was customary to read these charges at the making of a Mason.

Today few Masons have read these charges because they are no longer a part of our ritual. But in 1752 Masons were very familiar with these words (spelling modernized) from the second charge, entitled "Of the Civil Magistrate Supreme and Subordinate":

> A Mason is a peaceable subject to the civil powers, wherever he resides or works, and is never to be concerned in plots or conspiracies against the peace and welfare of the nation, nor to behave himself undutiful to inferior magistrates; for as Masonry hath been always injured by war, bloodshed, and confusion, so ancient kings and princes have been much disposed to encourage the craftsmen, because of their peaceableness and loyalty, whereby they practically answered the cavils of their adversaries, and promoted the honor of the fraternity, whoever flourished in times of peace. So that if a brother should be a rebel against the state, he is not to be countenanced in his rebellion, however he may be

pitied as an unhappy man; and if convicted of no other crime, though the loyal brotherhood must and ought to disown his rebellion, and give no umbrage or ground of political jealousy to the government for the time being; they cannot expel him from the lodge, and his relations to it remains indefensible."

Bro. George Washington, and every Mason who fought for the freedom of the colonies from Great Britain, knew this charge, and had to reconcile its mandate with what was manifestly a rebellion against the government to which he ostensibly owed his allegiance.

As such, it is important for us to remember that the decision to side with the colonists against the mother country, especially for Masons, was a serious one. Not only was there the danger that if the rebellion were lost that their lives would have been in jeopardy, but as Masons they also had to come to grips with the fundamental Masonic teaching that a brother "is not to be countenanced in his rebellion." In other words, the fraternity should not, and would not, encourage him to place himself in this unenviable position.

So how and why did Masons in the American Revolution come to the conclusion that they must foreswear the allegiance due to their king, and accept a new allegiance?

How did a man of sterling character such as George Washington reconcile the teachings of Freemasonry, which were so important to him, with the decision to lead the rebellion?

There were undoubtedly opportunists in the colonists' cause, but certainly George Washington and his fellow Masons were not among them. It was not opportunity that motivated them, but loyalty itself, as strange as that might seem. It was loyalty to their country—to their homeland —which caused them to choose the difficult and dangerous course of rebellion. For America had become their country—their homeland—and not Great Britain. It surely was the realization that the time had arrived in the course of history that a new nation should be born.

And for Masons, the second charge of 1723 provided the means of transferring their loyalty from the king to the people of America. For this curious charge explained that regardless of how painful such a decision would be, a Mason would not be expelled from Freemasonry if he chose to take this road to the future.

That is the real teaching of the second charge. While loyalty to one's obligations, including loyalty to the existing political arrangement, is important, there are sometimes things that are more important. In the case of the founding fathers who were Freemasons, it was the realization that their country was now America—and that the Freemasonry they loved would support them in this decision.

Washington, and others like him, had become Americans. It just took the Revolutionary War to make them realize it. And while Freemasons are loyal to the government under which they live, the lessons of the American Revolution provide evidence that there are times when allegiances must change.

Freemasons were present at the birth of America as a nation among nations of the world. One of the most difficult decisions that George Washington probably ever made was to become an American, and many think that Freemasonry helped him reach that difficult decision.

CHOICES
Freemasonry is all about choices

By John L. Cooper III
California Freemason, April - May 2010

A man has to make a deliberate choice to ask to become a Freemason in the first place, for no Mason will ask him to join.

He has to have made the right choices early in life—we call it being "under the tongue of good report"—before we can accept him into the fraternity. He then learns that Freemasonry will help him continue to make good choices by offering him an opportunity to shape his life according to its principal tenets and cardinal virtues. But the choice will still be his.

He learns that the journey will not always be an easy one. He will still all too often have to travel a "rough and rugged road."

At times he may wonder why he made Freemasonry his choice in life. In a world that often seems to reward those who "cheat, wrong, or defraud" others, he has promised never to do that. In a world that seems to care little for those at the bottom of the heap – those who find themselves on "the lowest spoke of fortune's wheel"—he always steps forward to help. When the path that others take leads them to the brink of disaster, he is there to point the way back home for them—an often thankless task.

And yet, for all that, he chose to become a Mason, and chooses to remain a Mason. Why?

He may never really know why he became a Mason. There was something that attracted him to a "band of brothers' who had chosen the same road, and who would travel with him to "that undiscovered country from whose bourn no traveler returns."

But he knows why he remains a Mason. It is a secret that is really no secret at all: He made a choice to take the road less traveled by, and "that has made all the difference."

Freemasonry is exclusive, not because those who belong to it are better than others, but because those who are Masons make better choices. And it all began at the beginning of the journey—at the beginning of his Masonic journey.

He chose to travel in the company of men who share his values, and who will be there to help him if he should stumble along the way. And he chose to "help, aid, and assist" those of his brethren along the way who need his strong hand in times of need. He chose to live a life

103

in which the only reward is the knowledge of a job well done, and the smile of those he reached out to help.

He chose to make a difference in the lives of others rather than living a self-centered life of ease.

He chose the "road not taken" by others, the "one less traveled by," because for him, "that has made all the difference."

A Progressive Moral Science

By John L. Cooper III
California Freemason, June - July 2010

The *Oxford English Dictionary* notes that the original meaning of science was "The state of fact of knowing; knowledge or cognizance of something specified or implied." It is in this sense that Freemasonry uses the term sciences to describe itself.

In the Fellow Craft degree we are reminded of the importance of making progress as a Mason. We use the term advanced to describe moving from being an Entered Apprentice Mason to becoming a Fellow Craft Mason, as in "Being advanced to the Second Degree of Freemasonry, I congratulate you on your preferment," the phrase in the charge that comes just before the new Fellow Craft is told that Freemasonry is a "progressive moral science."

If Freemasonry is defined in this context as a "progressive moral science," and the Fellow Craft is expected to advance as he becomes more conversant with it, then every Mason is bound to the same obligation. If so, then we should take a closer look at what it means to pursue advancement in an organization devoted to a body of knowledge defined as a "progressive moral science."

First, morals have to do with behavior. It is not an accident that the word morals is associated with mores, meaning customs, and with morale.

We use the term moral law to describe a list of morals that members of a community are expected to observe. Some are universal, being found in almost all societies, such as laws against theft or murder. Others may be specific to a particular society at a particular time, and over time become obsolete.

An example of the latter are sumptuary laws—laws regulating the consumption of luxury goods, and often intended to preserve social class distinctions. In the Massachusetts Bay Colony in colonial times, for example, only people with a personal fortune of at least 200 pounds were allowed to wear lace—a law which was soon ignored, and eventually disappeared from history.

It is in this sense that Freemasonry describes itself as a progressive moral science. In other words, Freemasons are expected to take a serious look at customs which may have no basis for their existence, and which may, in fact, be contrary to other and more valid ethical values, such as treating people equally regardless of social or economic status.

Secondly, Freemasonry acknowledges that we are bound to a greater law than mere custom. Our commitment to the concept of a Great Architect of the Universe implies that there is something more important than mere custom in defining that which is moral in the understanding of Freemasonry.

A commitment to something above and beyond ourselves means that we are bound by much more than just our own personal ideas as to what defines moral and what is beyond morality. Our understanding of the larger picture of morality is deeply intertwined with our belief in a God who looks beyond that which is mere convenience in our own simple definition of morality.

It is this commitment that prevents us from making morality simply a play upon words, and brings us into the presence of the One that enables us to reach beyond our own simple understanding of morality into a greater understanding outside of ourselves. To understand our commitment to God is to understand our commitment to morality in a way that we could not otherwise understand.

Freemasonry is, indeed, a science. It is a body of knowledge that enables us to approach God with a clear conscience. It is much more than a replication of customs from times past; It is a promise of the future to come. It is a "progressive science" because it is ever evolving, and because it brings us into the presence of God, whose understanding of morality is an ever-expanding application of the greatest gift He can give: that of love for others, and a brotherhood in which all men and women are created equal.

CONSIDER FREDERICK
From a despotic family and a war-torn country,
a Masonic king emerged

By John L. Cooper III
California Freemason, August - September 2010

On August 14, 1738, a man was initiated into Freemasonry in the middle of the night. The man—who was later to become Frederick the Great of Prussia—was one of the most influential men of his day.

Frederick was truly a renaissance man, whose love of art and music was impressive. He was also a military genius. When Napoleon Bonaparte visited Frederick's tomb at Potsdam, he was reported to have remarked, "Gentlemen, if this man were still alive, I would not be here!"

So famous a Mason was he that the Ancient and Accepted Scottish Rite counts him as a legendary founder of the rite through the Constitutions of 1786 – for which he was (erroneously) credited as author.

But his path to Masonry was not easy. Frederick inherited a backward country from a despotic and ill-tempered father. His initiation into Freemasonry in the middle of the night—actually at 2 a.m.—was directly a result of his father's opposition to his son becoming a Mason. Frederick tried to flee from his father, but was caught. His father forced him to watch his best friend, Hans Hermann von Katte, be executed as an accomplice in the plot to escape.

A man from such a family background might have ended up with one of the worst reputations in history instead of one of the best. Many Masonic historians think that it was Freemasonry itself that made the difference in Frederick the Great.

Frederick absorbed the teachings of Freemasonry, and had an unparalleled opportunity as the ruler of an emerging nation to translate his ideals into statecraft. In many respects, Frederick the Great was a Masonic king.

In the first degree of Masonry we are told that "...monarchs have, for a season, exchanged the scepter for the trowel, to patronize our mysteries and join in our assemblies." That might have described Frederick the Great more than any other monarch in the eighteenth century, and more than any other great leader of a nation, save for our own George Washington, who was a younger contemporary of Frederick the Great.

In addition to being a king and a military leader of genius, Frederick was known for his enlightened rule.

107

He promoted religious toleration at a time when it was not popular to do so. He encouraged fine architecture; Berlin still boasts many fine public buildings that were erected during his reign. He was a gifted musician, and composed more than one hundred sonatas for the flute, of which he was an expert player, as well as four symphonies. He had a close friendship with some of the greatest writers of the Enlightenment, including Voltaire – a fellow Freemason. In addition to his native German, Frederick spoke French, English, Spanish, Portuguese, and Italian, and understood and read Hebrew, Greek, and Latin.

Frederick tried to live up to his ideal of an enlightened monarch, following the model of the ancient Roman emperor and Stoic philosopher Marcus Aurelius. But he was also a military man of singular accomplishment.

His reign, to quote our ritual pertaining to the famous King David, father of King Solomon, was "one of many wars and much bloodshed." The unification of Germany a century later, essentially accomplished by another Prussian, Otto von Bismarck, would not have been possible had it not been for the military leadership of Frederick.

Frederick demonstrates that Freemasonry can create great leaders of war as well as great leaders of peace. He was a leader of both, and so history remembers a great Freemason who translated his Masonic ideals into the political reality of the dangerous world in which he lived.

The initiation of a Mason in the middle of the night on August 14, 1738, in Brunswick, Germany, had great implications for the future of the world.

BACK TO THE FUTURE
How would Masonry look today if history were rewritten?

By John L. Cooper III
California Freemason, October – November 2010

Many may remember the 1985 movie, *Back to the Future*, where a time traveler almost prevents his parents from meeting, a feat that would potentially eliminate his own existence. It was an amusing story, and while the logic may have been in doubt, the thesis was at least tenable.

Imagine, if you will, that some Masonic events of the past had turned out differently. Would we recognize the Freemasonry that might have resulted? Let's take a look.

In the beginning, Masonic lodges were casual affairs—at least they were in England. Although we have evidence of operative lodges in Scotland from early days, it seems as if lodges in England were created to "make a Mason," and then dissolved, never to meet again. We know that this is how Elias Ashmole was made a Mason in 1646 at Warrington, in Lancashire, because he wrote about it in his diary.

We know nothing of the ceremonies used, but apparently anyone who knew the ritual could convene a "lodge," and make a Mason. Had this practice prevailed, we would not have the kind of lodges that we know today, much less any of the rest of Freemasonry. There would be no grand lodge, no York Rite or Scottish Rite, no Eastern Star. All we would have would be some men who had been made Masons somewhere, sometime, with no connection to one another except having the common experience of a single, simple, ceremony.

What little we know about our early ceremonies of "making a Mason" shows that most of what we have in our three degrees today was not there in the beginning. There may have been Entered Apprentices, "Fellows," and perhaps some who were called "Master Masons," but there was virtually nothing to distinguish them from a ritual standpoint.

Had Freemasonry remained that way, the beauty of our ritual and lectures never would have descended to us.

There was no grand lodge until 1717, and when it was created, it was not for the purpose of governing the lodges nor for creating new ones. That had to await future developments. The original purpose, as found in our records, was to hold a banquet for the four original lodges. Grand lodge was originally a kind of "dinner committee" to plan the event!

In 1826 the Morgan Affair almost demolished Freemasonry entirely.

109

In the years that followed, we lost 60 percent of our members, and one grand lodge closed down entirely because it had no lodges left. Several states considered legislation that would have made it illegal to be a Mason. The damage to us was significant, but we survived, and in the following generation Freemasonry began once more to flourish in America.

When we look at the present we see the seeds of the future. In the 1990s it seemed as if Freemasonry in America was sliding down a steep and slippery slope to oblivion. Lodges were closing for lack of interest by their members; most only conferred degrees occasionally because they had no candidates. The average age of our members climbed as the fraternity became older without new and younger members.

Then suddenly things changed. Freemasonry was discovered by a new generation, and we began to grow once more. Lodges discovered that men wanted to become Masons, and they started conferring degrees once more. New lodges came into existence as Freemasonry began to climb out of the despondent 1990s into a new world after the turn of the twenty-first century. But what would have happened if that had not occurred?

Think for a moment if Freemasonry had not been ready for the surge of interest which broke upon us in recent years.

What if almost all our lodges had disappeared, so that there was nowhere that a man could apply for the degrees? What if our officers had forgotten the ritual, so that they could no longer make Masons? What if our lodges had been so unfriendly that they chased away all the men that were seeking us out?

What if the few remaining Masons had so little respect and love for Freemasonry that they didn't care if anyone else ever became a Mason? What if the lodges had become places of apathy and indolence, or places where members would rather quarrel with one another than practice the brotherhood that they were supposed to understand? What if no Masons were willing to recommend a man to become a Mason because they had no idea why they themselves were Masons?

Could it have happened in America? In California? In your lodge?

The future of Freemasonry is in our hands. Our ancestors made some good decisions that changed Freemasonry in a positive way so that it became the great fraternity that we cherish. Had they not done so, we would not have Freemasonry as we know it.

You and I are the "ancestors" of the future Masons. What are we doing to make Freemasonry flourish for them? What will they think if they, too, could come "back to the future"?

FROM A BADGE TO A SYMBOL
Emblems to allegories, Masonic symbols contain different levels of meaning

By John L. Cooper III
California Freemason, December –January 2011

Freemasons are easily identified in the public mind with the square and compass, with the letter G in the center. Not only does it appear on many of our buildings, but Masons wear it proudly on coats and jackets, as well as on rings. Even films such as *National Treasure* make use of the square and compass as a "brand," identifying us in the public eye as Freemasons.

Freemasons, however, have many such symbols, and nowhere in our ritual is there a statement that the square and compass is our primary symbol. Indeed, it is not our primary symbol, regardless of its widespread public use.

The primary badge identifying a Mason is the white lambskin apron. At the very beginning of his Masonic journey, we tell an Entered Apprentice: "[The lambskin apron] is an emblem of innocence and the badge of a Mason."

Many Masons wear name badges—badges that identify them as members of a particular lodge, or as holders of a particular office in Masonry. These badges proclaim to others that we are a part of something larger than ourselves, and/or that we have been entrusted with something more important than just a simple membership. But such badges have little to do with the true "badge" of a Mason.

The true badge, we are told, is also an emblem—an emblem of innocence.

When presented with the lambskin apron, we are told for the first time that it has an inner as well as an outer meaning. Like the name badge, the lambskin apron identifies us to the world at large as Masons.

But it carries a meaning far deeper than that of a mere badge, and that is the meaning of the term emblem.

An emblem goes beyond a badge and enters into the world of symbolism. The white lambskin apron is therefore both a badge for others to know us as Masons and a symbol of something much deeper, something that turns our thoughts inward rather than outward. It reminds us that we are engaged in a great enterprise, which has far more meaning to each of us as individuals than it can ever have for the world at large. The lambskin apron is an outward and visible symbol of an inward and spiritual grace.

The use of such symbols to turn our thoughts toward God, and to our own spiritual values, is very old. Carvings in stone at Tell el Amarna in Egypt show a solar disk with hands extended in blessing. The purpose was to show that what the Egyptians perceived as the source of all life—the sun—was also the source of continual good things to men and women on earth. But this emblem was much more than just a reminder of the solar energy that makes all life possible. It was a symbol of God – one of the first representations of a monotheistic God in history.

In a similar fashion, the lambskin apron is a symbol of the blessings of God that we seek in our work as Masons. Shortly after an Entered Apprentice is presented with his very own white lambskin apron, he is taught an important lesson about Masonic progress toward "perfection." Later in the evening he is told that two important symbols for a Mason, taken from our stonemason ancestors, are the rough ashlar and the perfect ashlar. An ashlar is a rectangular block of hewn stone.

Stonemasons use rectangular blocks of stone in building a wall because of the stability that they lend to the finished structure. Each row of rectangular blocks of stone is placed so that each stone overlaps the one below it, keeping the blocks tightly fitted against one another. The rough ashlar is the beginning of the process of building the wall; the perfect ashlar is the end product—a stone made so smooth on all sides that the cement uniting the blocks will adhere uniformly to the surfaces, and provide a lasting bond.

The perfect ashlar is not an emblem of absolute perfection in some abstract sense, but is as perfect as the stonemason can make it for the purposes intended. The perfect ashlar is a symbol of making our lives fit into that spiritual building which Masons are building—lives that are useful for creating a stable and lasting structure for the benefit of humanity.

Both the white lambskin apron and the perfect ashlar are often misunderstood by those who do not truly understand Freemasonry. Neither the apron nor the ashlar implies that a Mason will become a perfect man, free of all defects and untouched by sin. The concept of perfection amongst Masons is not a theological concept. Freemasonry makes no statement about religion, and makes no promise that by wearing the lambskin apron or shaping his life into a perfect ashlar, he will thereby gain admission into heaven. Those concepts are the province of religion, and not Freemasonry.

We use these symbols, instead, as a way of explaining that our lives here on Earth must be truly useful to God, and to our fellow humans, if they are to have value in this earthly life. If we allow our white lambskin apron to become soiled and dirty because of the way in which we live our lives, others will notice. If we leave our rough-hewn ashlar in that state for a lifetime, our work will be of little value in building a stable and useful society. These symbols of Freemasonry encourage us to take a look at what we are doing with our lives, and to work to improve our contribution to the building of that "house not made with hands, eternal in the heavens."

Freemasonry teaches by symbol and by allegory. As important as the square and compass are to us as Masons, they are not our primary symbols. The white lambskin apron is. It teaches us that the world will notice what we do with our lives, and that our efforts to preserve unsullied this primary emblem of a Mason are also tied to the usefulness of what we do as Masons.

It is only at the end of our life that we will truly understand why we were told that it is "more honorable than the Star or Garter, or any distinction that can be conferred...." If worthily worn, it is most certainly "an emblem of innocence, and the badge of a Mason...." But it is more. Above all our symbols, it is the only one that we continually wear with "honor to the Fraternity" as well as "pleasure to ourselves."

THE INDISSOLUBLE CHAIN

To relieve the distressed is a duty incumbent on all men, but particularly on Masons, who are linked together by an indissoluble chain of sincere affection

By John L. Cooper III
California Freemason, February – March 2011

In the lecture of the first degree of Masonry, we encounter for the first time the symbol of the chain. The chain is one of the more neglected symbols of Masonry, but that should not be so. It is, in fact, one of the more powerful symbols through which Masonry teaches an important lesson. It actually has many meanings in Masonry, but in this context, it is associated with "a duty incumbent on all men, but particularly on Masons..." In order to truly understand our obligation "to relieve the distressed," we need to understand the meaning of the Masonic chain.

The first aspect of this symbol, and perhaps the most easily understood, is that a chain is composed of separate links. In the lecture, relief – the second of the three principal tenets of Freemasonry – follows that of brotherly love, which is the first. The placement is purposeful. Without understanding the dimension of brotherly love, a Mason would have little concept of the chain that links him to other Masons. The chain of Freemasonry is not the chain of the prisoner nor of the slave; is it the voluntary assuming of a link in the chain of brotherhood, which one has promised to support of his "own free will and accord." The chain that binds him to his brethren will only be broken by death, but it is still voluntary.

It is this brotherly love to which the "indissoluble chain of sincere affection" refers. The obligation to relieve the distressed grows out of the Mason's understanding of this brotherly love, which encompasses not only other Masons, but also their families and – by extension – any who are in need.

There is, however, a deeper symbolism of the chain within Freemasonry. According to some Masonic writers, it is associated with the "silver cord" of life itself, and with the cabletow, the other symbol of brotherhood. In the Masonic memorial service, we make reference to the fact that death has "loosed" the silver cord. We also make reference to the fact that a link in the chain binding a Mason to his brethren has been broken. The "lost link" is related to relief; having passed beyond this earthly life, the "chain of sincere affection" has been broken, and this has, in turn, altered forever the possibility of the brother continuing to extend relief to others.

Or has it? The very nature of a chain is that broken links can be, and are, replaced. Every new Mason who assumes his obligation as an Entered Apprentice Mason becomes a new link in the chain. Even if a link is broken, the chain of brotherhood is not. In fact we explain this to the candidate when we inform him that "the greatest of these is charity… [for] charity extends beyond the grave, through the boundless realms of eternity." Indeed it does. The ability to extend relief does not, therefore, cease with our individual ability to extend it, but rather continues because the chain itself is renewed through the addition of new links.

In some times and in some places, Masons have assembled around the altar at the closing of the lodge and joined hands in a symbolic representation of this "chain of sincere affection." It is a powerful symbol that when we leave the lodge, and "return to our respective places of abode," as the ritual says, that we will shortly return to the world where Freemasonry will be practiced by our individual efforts. The chain is not broken, even though we drop hands with a brother, because the chain that binds us together can never be broken, until death brings about the final separation. But we are reminded upon leaving the lodge that we have a duty to perform. We are to perform the duty that is incumbent upon all men – but particularly upon Masons.

From this understanding have arisen the great Masonic charities with which the world is familiar. We have built homes for the aged and infirm amongst us; we have offered medical services to children in need; we have given scholarships so that young people may learn; and we have done much, much more. We demonstrate that relief is not an idle principle for Masons. It is one of the three essential characteristics of a Mason.

May the symbol of the chain remain a powerful and important one in our understanding of Freemasonry!

THE CITADEL OF OUR SAFETY
Public education's power to unite

By John L. Cooper III
California Freemason, April – May 2011

The power of Masonic ritual lies, in part, in the indelible imprint that it makes on our minds and hearts. Some ritual is so memorable that we seem never to forget it, because the imagery speaks to us in ways that touch us in our deepest being. And not all such ritual is, strictly speaking, Masonic. Some comes to us from sources that have been inspired by Freemasonry. Those of us who began our journey as members of the Order of DeMolay understand this well. Although the DeMolay ritual is very young by Masonic standards, it speaks to us across the years in a very special way.

When the officers of a DeMolay chapter are installed, the installing officer explains to them, and to all those present, something about the teachings of the Order of DeMolay. In a very real sense, the installation service (as DeMolay terms it) contains a summary of what Freemasons want these young men to know about the teachings of the order, and one image, in particular, has meant a great deal to me as a public school teacher.

At an appropriate moment in the installation, the installing officer walks to the DeMolay altar in the center of the room, and says the following:

> From the station in the East, emblematic of the morning years of life, we place the school books on the Altar as a symbol of the intellectual liberty, without which there could be neither civil nor religious freedom. They are particularly emblematic of the great public school system of our country, the foundation of that universal enlightenment which is the crowning glory of our institutions. Devoted championship of our public schools is a cardinal teaching of the Order of DeMolay. We are unalterably opposed to the same building housing a school, a church and a seat of civil government. Civil, religious and intellectual liberty are the three sources of our country's greatness, but they must stand alone, upon separate foundations and under separate roofs. These books, representative of those being carried to and from the public schools by millions of boys and girls each day, are just as vital symbols of our liberties as the Holy Bible, which is the rule and

117

guide of our faith, or the flag which protects the church, the school and the seat of civil power. We, therefore, place these books upon the Altar and I solemnly enjoin the members of this Chapter ever to stand unswervingly for the protection and perpetuity of the free public schools, the citadel of our safety and the source of the only real freedom possible in a government of the people, by the people and for the people.

The phrase "the citadel of our safety" is a very powerful image in this collection of powerful images. We live in a world in which safety has become ever more important. Whether it is the sacrifices of those who stand guard over our freedoms on distant shores, or the "thin blue line" closer to home, we understand the need for safety in order to live our lives of peace and prosperity. These protections—and these protectors—are easy to understand. But what about the public schools as the "citadel" of our safety? What image does that create for us? And how do the public schools do that? Let me share some thoughts.

First, what the image does not mean. As important as the educated mind is to Freemasonry (the Fellow Craft degree is all about this subject), that is not exactly a citadel. Secondly, it is not about schools. Freemasonry has no quarrel with private schools, and does not object to those who send their children to private schools if they wish to do so. And it is not an unthinking and uncritical support for anything and everything that goes on in our public schools. Freemasons can, and do, differ on how they think the public schools should be funded, how they should teach, and how they should respond to the challenges presented to them by a diverse society. The "citadel of our safety" has nothing to do with these issues. It is, instead, something else—something much more profound.

Freemasonry has long recognized that no society can long survive unless its citizens are capable of governing themselves. And it recognizes that no society can long survive unless its citizens share a common culture that binds them together in a common enterprise, regardless of political, social, and religious differences. For Freemasons, the public schools are the center of this commitment to the fostering of a common culture, which unites us into one family of Americans. The public schools are at the center of our community, and even when families choose to send their children to schools other than the public schools, those local public schools still symbolically stand for this unity, which must be accepted by all. The public schools are the yardstick by which non-public schools are measured. No community in America is without its public school, and it stands for the safety of our unity as Americans in a way that no other institution can.

Our public schools are not the creature of any religious system, nor are they, strictly speaking, "government," even if they are publicly funded and guided by elected representatives of the people. They are separate, as the DeMolay ritual says so well. Our schools symbolically stand on separate

118

foundations, and under separate roofs. And Freemasonry stands for the "protection and perpetuity" of our public schools because as Freemasons we understand why this must be so in a government "of the people, by the people, and for the people."

INQUIRING MINDS WANT TO KNOW
The 39 exposés – and counting – that shape Masonry

By John L. Cooper III
California Freemason, June –July 2011

How many exposures of the ritual of Freemasonry have there been? Coil's Encyclopedia lists 39. That is an incredible number for an organization whose rituals are supposed to be held in strictest secrecy. Some of these exposés are better known than others, and tell us important things about our history.

The first comprehensive exposure was published in 1730 in London. There had been others before, but Prichard's *Masonry Dissected* was the first that contained all three degrees with which we are now familiar.

Prichard claimed to be a member of a London lodge, but if so, he didn't name it, and the lodge has never been discovered. Analysis of *Masonry Dissected* leads us to believe that it substantially represents the ritual as it existed in 1730. We know that the 20 years before had been a seminal period for Masonic ritual, as it evolved from a simple admission ceremony to the three degrees that we know today. *Masonry Dissected* consists of a series of questions and answers for each of the three degrees, and not the kind of ritual that we know today. It actually consists of the degree lectures used in those days; not the narrative lectures with which we are familiar today, but the candidate's proficiency lectures.

The next significant exposure was actually a set published in 1760 and 1762. The first, *Three Distinct Knocks*, purported to be the ritual used by the Moderns, while the second, *Jachin and Boaz*, represented itself as the ritual of the Ancients. They are both so similar that it is likely that the second one was copied from the first, and so we are still not sure how the ritual of the Ancients differed from that of the Moderns. The significance of these two exposures is that for the first time we find a Masonic lodge that we would recognize today. Deacons appear for the first time, and some of the ritual is in narrative format.

Perhaps the most famous exposé of all was that published by William Morgan in 1826, and which led to his kidnapping and presumed murder.

As with Prichard, we don't know when or where Morgan was made a Mason, or even if he was a Mason at all. He showed up in Batavia, New York, in 1825, and got involved in local Masonic activities. Although a ne'er-do-well, he had the gift of gab, and soon wormed his way into the local lodges. He also got himself invited to join the local Royal Arch chapter —in those days a significant honor. However, he got crosswise with the local Masons, and decided to make money out of his knowledge of the rituals by publishing and selling them.

It was this decision that led to his being jailed and kidnapped, and to his subsequent disappearance. As the story goes, Morgan was jailed on trumped-up charges of owing a debt. To prevent the publication of the rituals, Masons from the local lodges freed him from jail and carried him off. At the later trial they claimed that they had taken him across the border to Canada and released him. But he never returned.

This episode caused an uproar in New York, which quickly spread across the country. Masons were accused of being a subversive society which must be stamped out. Their reputation in some communities was very much like that of al-Qaida terrorists today. Men resigned from Freemasonry in droves, and lodges closed for lack of members. The Grand Lodge of Vermont even ceased to function because all its lodges went dark.

Although no one has ever learned the truth about Morgan and his disappearance, it took more than 20 years before Freemasonry began to recover from this disaster. The rituals were actually published, despite Morgan's disappearance. His business partner printed and sold the rituals, and copies are still available today—including a Kindle edition.

Why all the exposés? Nowadays we have dues receipts to identify a visiting Mason, and if there is any doubt about identity, we can always ask for a picture I.D. We supplement this by asking him to prove that he knows something about Freemasonry by answering certain questions, posed by the examining committee. These questions are often perfunctory nowadays, but in the eighteenth century, they were very important. There was no other way to prove that a visitor had truly been made a Mason in a proper lodge. The exposures revealed the answers to most of the questions that were normally asked of a visitor in those days, and thus anyone who took the trouble to memorize some of the questions and answers from one of the exposés could worm his way into a lodge.

Some exposés were published by disaffected Masons who were angry at Masonry for some reason, and decided to publish the secret rituals to punish the fraternity. Some were published and sold for financial gain: The public was interested in what Masons were doing behind closed doors, and were willing to buy copies to find out.

Other exposures originated in "crib notes," written down to help a Mason remember the ritual. Some of these found their way into other hands, and were published. Some were published in code, much like our current cipher ritual, so that there would be a comprehensive copy of the ritual written down so that changes would not be made inadvertently.

At a later stage a decision was made to print some of the ritual in plain text—the origin of our monitorial work – so that only some parts of the ritual would be considered secret.

How did Masons cope with all these exposures? Thankfully, most did not resort to the drastic measure of kidnapping the author and causing him to disappear. In most cases, they simply ignored them. After all, if Masons didn't say anything to confirm or deny an exposé, how would anyone know if it was accurate? However, in 1723 another tactic was tried, which was one of the more creative responses to the problem.

In 1999, prominent Masonic scholar S. Brent Morris presented a paper at the A. Douglas Smith, Jr. Lodge of Research No. 1949 in Alexandria, Va. While in London some years before, he had come across one of the early exposures, published in 1723 in one of the popular newspapers of the day, *The Post Boy*. It purported to be an exposé of the ritual of Freemasonry, one of several similar such publications around that time.

But Bro. Morris noticed that while some of the questions were similar to other such questions in circulation, some of them were peculiar. He made an exhaustive study of all the exposures on a question-by-question basis, and concluded that the one published in *The Post Boy* was a deliberate attempt to mislead those who were using the exposures to gain admission to a lodge. In other words, this was a "disinformation" project that some Masons had concocted in order to purposely lead astray those who tried to use this information to gain admission to a lodge. It was a brilliant ploy, and one that must have confounded those who thought that they would use the exposé to get inside a Masonic lodge! The project was using the exposures against their best customers, and it is likely that upon finding out that the information was worthless, the purchase of other such exposures diminished.

The story of Masonic exposures is a complex one, and in the long run they never posed a real threat to Freemasonry—with the single exception of the William Morgan episode of 1826. Students of Freemasonry use the exposures to gain a glimpse that they would otherwise not have into the rituals of earlier times. However, the basic questions as to their validity and accuracy still remain. And as long as Masons keep their obligation to keep the rituals secret, we will probably never know how accurate any of them really were. So it is that even today, Masons keep the public guessing as to what we are really doing in our lodges!

DEATH OF A CRAFTSMAN
The legend and lessons behind a famous work of craftsmanship

By John L. Cooper III
California Freemason, August – September 2011

In Rosslyn Chapel, in Scotland, stands a memorial to the remarkable skill of the stonemason's art. Called the Apprentice Pillar, it might also be called the Pillar of Beauty, for it is an exquisite example of freestone carving by an operative mason. The legend, which may not be as old as the pillar itself, tells of the tragic end of the craftsman who carved it, and the jealousy that caused his murder.

It begins with a Master Mason who assigns an Entered Apprentice the task of carving the third, and most beautiful, of the central pillars in the chapel. He does not give the Entered Apprentice any instruction in how to carve the pillar, perhaps because he wants the Entered Apprentice to fail at the task.

The Master Mason then sets off for a foreign land, ostensibly to study a famous pillar and then bring the design back to the chapel, where he will complete the pillar that the failed Entered Apprentice could not carve. However, upon his return, he discovers that the Entered Apprentice has completed the pillar, and that he has done so with a skill that the Master Mason could never hope to achieve. In his anger, the Master Mason strikes the Entered Apprentice on the forehead with a setting maul, felling him dead at his feet.

As a punishment for his crime, the other stonemasons carve a stone head representing the Master Mason along the inner wall of the chapel, with its gaze forever fixed on the Apprentice Pillar. And across from this, they carve another head—one representing the slain Entered Apprentice, with a great wound on his forehead, gazing forever at the stone head of his murderer. The crime and its consequences were carved in stone for all time.

Regardless of whether this legend has any basis in fact, the beautiful Apprentice Pillar is still in Rosslyn Chapel, and the stone heads are still looking on after all these centuries. There is a Masonic allusion in this tale, but there is also a deeper Masonic significance in what the story tells us.

The legend is about the failure of the Master Mason to perform his prime duty of instructing his Entered Apprentice, and, instead, plotting to discredit him and claim the glory for himself. It backfires, and instead of our remembering the great skill of the Master Mason, we remember only his betrayal. The beauty created by the Entered Apprentice is his lasting memorial.

The story teaches three Masonic lessons that we should not forget. First, it is the duty of every Mason to empower another Mason to succeed. Every Entered Apprentice is told that his "future moral and Masonic edifice" will be built well and truly if he stays close to the "master builder" in his lodge – symbolically represented by the master of the lodge. That, in turn, requires the master to teach Freemasonry to those in his charge, and particularly to a new Mason.

Second, we are taught to circumscribe our passions, and keep them within due bounds. Focused energy is a blessing; unfocused anger and rage is destructive of all societies, and especially of ours. Jealousy has no place in Freemasonry, for—as we are taught—a Mason only succeeds in an environment of those who can work together and agree.

Finally, there is another lesson that comes from this old legend of Rosslyn Chapel and its Entered Apprentice Pillar: the lesson of doing what we are expected to do in the best way that we can, regardless of the consequences. It is possible that the Entered Apprentice knew that he would be in trouble if he completed carving the pillar that the Master Mason had expected to complete himself. But he did so because he wanted to create a thing of beauty. That urge overrode any other possibility.

I am reminded of a beautiful poem by Kent M. Keith, which supposedly hung on the wall of Mother Teresa's home in Calcutta, India:

> People are often unreasonable, illogical, and self-centered;
> Forgive them anyway.
> If you are kind, people may accuse you of selfish, ulterior motives;
> Be kind anyway.
> If you are successful, you will win some false friends and some true enemies;
> Succeed anyway.
> If you are honest and frank, people may cheat you;
> Be honest and frank anyway.
> What you spend years building, someone could destroy overnight;
> Build anyway.
> If you find serenity and happiness, they may be jealous;
> Be happy anyway.
> The good you do today, people will often forget tomorrow;
> Do good anyway.
> Give the world the best you have, and it may never be enough;
> Give the world the best you've got anyway.
> You see, in the final analysis, it is between you and your God;
> It was never between you and them anyway.

As the Entered Apprentice of old carved his pillar because it was the best that he could contribute to his beautiful chapel, so we as Masons contribute the best that we can every day to the betterment of the world around us. Regardless of the consequences, he carved his pillar anyway, and regardless of the consequences, we, too, live as Masons should anyway.

THE MASONIC EXPLORER
Whither are you traveling?

By John L. Cooper III
California Freemason, October – November 2011

There is an old question asked of a Mason at an important point in his Masonic life: "Whence came you and whither are you traveling?" When the question is asked, there is not much time for contemplation. The question is answered quickly, and ritualistically—and then often forgotten as the more dramatic sequel in the ritual captures our attention. It is too bad, in a way, that we cannot stop at this point—our ceremonies and take time to think about the question and formulate an answer which is specific to each Mason who is asked it. "Where are you coming from?" And—knowing what you now know about Freemasonry—"Where are you going?"

There is an old joke about Christopher Columbus which is singularly unfair to him, but which nonetheless is still being told. In one form it goes like this: "When he started out, he didn't know where he was going. When he got there he didn't know where he was. And when he got home he didn't know where he had been." The joke is unfair because anyone who has the courage to strike out into the unknown is to be commended, not ridiculed. The courageous do not stay home. They go forth to places that they have never known before because of the challenge that it presents. And when they arrive, they have to incorporate all their previous experience into making the new "present" understandable. And this new "present" may take years, if not many generations, to truly understand. When the courageous return home with new information they may never know how great an impact their courage has made on the future.

In a sense, we are asking each Mason to have the courage to seek a future that he cannot yet know. Our symbolic way of expressing this is "Whither are you traveling?", but what we are really asking is, "Do you have the courage to seek out the unknown toward which Freemasonry points?" Freemasonry is a journey, and when a man stands for the first time at its gate—the West Gate—he cannot know where that journey will lead. We present him with tools and implements to use along the way, but we do not tell him how to use them. He must figure that out for himself. He is surrounded by "friends and brothers" at the beginning of the journey, but there will be a time when he will be alone, and when he must discover the way forward without any guidance—except for the guidance of the Supreme Architect of the Universe. He learns that the road ahead will

129

not always be smooth. It will sometimes be a "rough and rugged" road, one filled with dangers, real or imaginary, but dangers nonetheless. Only courage will cause him to begin the journey, and only courage will cause him to pursue the journey's end, even when assailed by forces stronger than he is, which may, in the end, prove fatal.

Masons should frequently ask themselves the question that was once posed to them: "Whither are you traveling?" It will take courage to ask it, for it is easier to drift through life without answering the question than it is to accept its challenge. But in the end, the journey's end, it will be worth it. The words from Robert Frost's poem, "The Road Not Taken" say it all:

> I shall be telling this with a sigh
> Somewhere ages and ages hence:
> Two roads diverged in a wood, and I,
> I took the one less traveled by,
> And that has made all the difference.

How Does Your Garden Grow?
In Freemasonry, we find the beauty of life itself

By John L. Cooper III
California Freemason, December - January 2012

In some respects, Freemasonry is like a beautiful garden. A garden is a living entity that brings beauty to the eye of the beholder. Some gardens are formal, with flower beds laid out with regularity, and whose charm lies in the order and symmetry thus displayed. Some gardens are informal, looking as if God had cast seeds to the earth in random order, but whose composite beauty when in bloom defies description. Freemasonry is like such a garden—or rather, like a constellation of gardens, all presenting a different aspect to the eye of the beholder.

As with a formal garden, there are aspects of our fraternity that we cherish which are formal in nature. Our degrees, conferred with exactness of word and ceremony, convey the timeless lessons that all Masons learn as they pass through them. Our meetings impose the formality of respect for the presiding officer, and through him, respect for all brethren present. We have the ancient teachings of Freemasonry enshrined in our lectures, which convey timeless truths to each generation.

But Freemasonry also shares the exuberance of the wilder garden, where color and shape run riot. There is friendship, which knows no bounds of formality, but which spills over into a cascade of good deeds, done without hope of fee or reward. There is brotherly love, which constrains not only our relationships with one another, but inspires our commitment to our families, friends, and neighbors. It fills our idle hours with pleasure, and undergirds and supports our busier hours as wage earner, citizen, and perhaps, as husband and father. We find in Freemasonry a deep sense of the beauty of life itself, and our ancient and honorable institution becomes the source of great personal satisfaction as the years roll by.

To ask a Mason why he is a Mason is analogous to asking a gardener why he gardens. A gardener finds in his garden a sense of order and beauty, and an expectation of the unanticipated that only the Master Gardener can bring into being. Similarly, a Mason finds in his fraternity the peace and serenity of sincere friendship and brotherhood, a sense of order and harmony as set forth in the principles of Freemasonry, and the surprise of joy when Freemasonry opens to him a vista that he never knew existed. To explain why membership in this ancient brotherhood is so valuable to a Mason is easy. Just look around.

Novus Ordo Seclorum
Masonic principles pointed the way for a new republic

By John L. Cooper III
California Freemason, February – March 2012

The role of Freemasonry in the founding of the United States of America is well known. Not only were some of the leading Founding Fathers members of the craft, but the principles of Freemasonry were instrumental in the intellectual and social revolution that led to the Declaration of Independence, with its ringing statement: "We hold these truths to be self-evident, that all men are created equal, that they are endowed by their Creator with certain unalienable Rights, that among these are Life, Liberty and the pursuit of Happiness."

Not so well known, however, is the role that Freemasonry played in the formative years of the American republic. On Dec. 24, 1793, Bro. DeWitt Clinton was installed as master of Holland Lodge No. 8 in New York City. In his inaugural address as master, he said the following:

> It is well known that our Order was at first composed of scientific and ingenious men who assembled to improve the arts and sciences, and cultivate a pure and sublime system of morality. Knowledge at that time, was restricted to a chosen few; but when the invention of printing had opened the means of instruction to all ranks of people, then the generous cultivators of Masonry communicated with cheerfulness to the world those secrets of the arts and sciences which had been transmitted and improved from the foundation of the institutions[.] [Our Fraternity then bent its] principal attention to the cultivation of morality. And Masonry may now be defined as a moral institution, intended to promote individual and social happiness.

Clinton went on to become a United States senator and the sixth governor of the state of New York. In 1812 he was the Federalist Party candidate for president, although he was defeated by James Madison. He was also the father of the Erie Canal. In his inaugural address, Clinton was expressing sentiments that would become the foundation of Freemasonry's association with the new American republic.

In his book *Revolutionary Brotherhood*, author Steven C. Bullock notes that:

Moral training had been a goal of Masonry since its creation, but post-Revolutionary Americans gave this activity powerful new ideological meaning. Virtue, the rejection of self-interest in favor of moral rules and the good of the whole, seemed to provide the essential foundation of a republican society. Leaders had always required self-control to withstand the temptations of power and corruption. But republics, unlike monarchical or aristocratic governments, did not depend solely upon their leaders. The people's character ultimately determined the health and prosperity of a society without the strong government and traditional restraints that had previously undergirded the social order. And many post-Revolutionary Americans feared that virtue could not be sustained, allowing the Republic to degenerate into either despotism or anarchy. George Washington's 1796 Farewell Address thus called morality one of the "great Pillars of human happiness" and "political prosperity." Masonry helped to provide the foundation for this building, training and teaching Americans to reinforce "the duties of men and Citizens." As Washington noted to his brothers only a few months later, America needed to become what Masonry already was: 'a lodge for the virtues.'

Non-Masons have often speculated whether the motto of the United States of America, found on the Great Seal—"Novus Ordo Seclorum"—has any Masonic significance. It has—but one that few Masonic authors have noticed.

Anti-Masons are fond of suggesting that this phrase means that Freemasonry is a secret conspiracy to create a world government under its control, and that the United States of America was the first step in this process. That is nonsense. But it is quite accurate to say that Freemasons were hoping that the United States of America would become a "new order of the ages," a republic that would not "degenerate into either despotism or anarchy," as Bullock noted.

Only a few months after leaving the office of president of the United States, Bro. George Washington responded to a request from the Grand Lodge of Pennsylvania for his views on Freemasonry and the new American republic. It was from his reply that Steven Bullock has quoted an excerpt, above. However, President Washington's full remarks on this occasion are worth noting:

> Fellow Citizens and Brothers of the Grand Lodge of Pennsylvania: I have received your address with all the feelings of brotherly affection, mingled with those sentiments for the society which it was calculated to excite. To have been

in any degree an instrument in the hands of Providence to promote order and union, and erect, upon solid foundation, the true principles of government, is only to have shared with many others in a labour, the result of which, let us hope, will prove through all ages, a Sanctuary for Brothers and a Lodge for the Virtues.

Our first president is not here expressing a hope that Freemasons will govern the new republic; far from it. What he is expressing is the hope that the principles that guide Freemasonry will undergird the new country in such a manner that America will become a place where brotherhood is the hallmark of citizenship, and where virtues will find a home.

The United States of America—the world's first large-scale democratic republic—has survived to become the paradigm of freedom because these Masonic lessons became a part of the fabric of the new American republic. This is the true Masonic "secret" that we passed on to the United States of America at its founding. And so it has been for more than 200 years. The American republic was truly a "New Order of the Ages."

A Novel Idea
American Masonry establishes Masonic youth orders

By John L. Cooper III
California Freemason, April – May 2012

As America emerged from World War I, it was evident that the world had changed. The war that had been supposed to make the world safe for democracy, had instead shown that the immense sacrifice of so many lives had turned the world upside down. Recoiling from the horrors of the first modern war, Americans began to turn inward, looking for strength in their own social institutions, and for a means of rebuilding their lives in a new era. Freemasonry was not left out of this change. Before World War I it had been a rather conventional men's fraternity, sharing the stage with numerous other fraternal orders which dominated the social life of American men. After World War I it emerged as the pre-eminent men's fraternity in America, easily displacing in popularity all its rivals. It set about building magnificent new buildings across the civic landscape, and achieved a high point of popularity which it had not enjoyed since the aftermath of the American Revolution.

Freemasonry had now also become a family institution, with the growing popularity of the Order of the Eastern Star. The new buildings had space set aside for the Order of the Eastern Star, with their emblems prominently displayed, and the new equality of women in society—a product of World War I—meant that men and women were sharing the ethos of Freemasonry in a new and vibrant way.

It was out of this that the Masonic youth orders came into existence. The first of these, the Order of DeMolay, was originally created in 1919 out of a baseball team of Masonic orphans in Kansas City, Missouri. It was soon followed by other youth orders, two of which survived to become the International Order of Job's Daughters, and the International Order of Rainbow for Girls. With the advent of these youth orders, Freemasonry completed its transformation from a men's fraternal order to a "family of Freemasonry," a Freemasonry that was much more than just a male-only society, but rather one that brought into its orbit wives and children of Masons.

There were other youth organizations in America, of course. Both the Boy Scouts and the Girl Scouts were growing in strength in the 1920's, and churches promoted organizations of youth as a means of encouraging them to become active members in later years as adults. But the Masonic youth orders were unique. They combined two things from Freemasonry which set them apart from other similar organizations. The first was the use of the initiatic process, and ritual, to create a lasting impression on the minds and hearts of teenagers, and the second was to teach young people to lead their own organizations. Just as the liberation of women to take an equal place in society with men had been a result of World War I, so the novel idea that young people could learn to govern themselves was unique. All three of the youth orders adopted a model of teaching youth to make good decisions by shaping the environment in which decisions are made, and providing adult support for young people to make good decisions on their own.

It should have not been surprising that this development occurred first within Freemasonry. Freemasonry has had a long history of developing "cutting edge" ideas, which later become an accepted part of society. Dr. Margaret Jacob, the prominent historian of Freemasonry in the eighteenth century, has pointed out that Masonic lodges were places where civil society first learned democratic practices—practices which were then copied by emerging democratic governments, such as the United States. In the nineteenth century Freemasons established public schools and non-sectarian colleges, which later became universal features of modern nations. And in the twentieth century, Freemasonry pioneered the idea that our youth could learn to lead through taking responsibility for their own organizations, and learn to make sound decisions in life by being surrounded by teachings which encourage right thinking. DeMolay, Job's Daughters, and Rainbow did it first in the 1920's, and they do it today.

Job's Daughters uses the story of Job from the Bible to teach lessons of steadfastness in the face of adversity, of faithfulness to commitments made, and respect for others. Rainbow has a constellation of ideals from which spring good actions—ideals such as love, religion, and nature. DeMolays are taught the importance of seven virtues: filial love, reverence for sacred things, courtesy, comradeship, fidelity, cleanness and patriotism. All three youth orders learn that we find our greatest meaning when we serve others, and all are engaged in charitable outreach to improve the world around them. And all three are rooted in Freemasonry, and are a part of the "family of Freemasonry" which first flourished in the years after World War I.

Freemasonry today continues in its tradition of first developing an idea, and then sharing it with the world. The Masonic youth orders are an example of this long tradition. This novel idea has spread around the world, for the Masonic youth orders now find a place in many other countries. The idea that young people can learn to make good decisions by learning to do so in an environment rich in idealism, and learning to govern themselves by doing it in a place where caring and committed adults help them to do so, has made a definite impact on our world – an impact for good. Freemasons can be proud of their support for our Masonic youth orders not only for what it does to help young people grow up to become responsible and caring leaders for tomorrow, but for what the idea has contributed to our society as a whole. The proverb attributed to King Solomon is instructive: "Train up a child in the way he should go, and when he is old he will not depart from it."

Masonic Parades as Street Theater
A Mason's behavior in the 'theater' of life is ever important

By John L. Cooper III
California Freemason, June – July 2012

In an issue of this magazine devoted to the performing arts, it is interesting to note, that in the eighteenth century one of the most famous controversies in Freemasonry involved what we can term "Freemasonry as theater." Here is the story.

As Freemasonry emerged into the public light in London in the years after 1717, Masons discovered a love of parading in public in their aprons and other Masonic regalia. This habit quickly gave them a publicity that they apparently enjoyed. Today, when Masons join a parade they usually receive a very positive response. We encourage lodges to make their presence known by appearing in parades, and who can resist cheering when a Shriners marching unit goes by?

The reaction of the public in the eighteenth century, however, was quite different. At first, curious about these men in their white aprons marching out of taverns through the crowded streets of London, some started to laugh at this strange sight. It wasn't long before groups of citizens began to form parades to mock the Masons. We have newspaper accounts of these mocking parades in the streets of London in the 1720s and 1730s, lampooning the Masons and making fun of their weird garb. Finally the Grand Lodge had enough, and enacted a regulation forbidding lodges to parade in public without express permission from the grand master.

It is here that the story takes a different turn. A celebrated Mason, William Preston, was master of one of the four old lodges which had formed the Grand Lodge in London in 1717. His lodge, later called the Lodge of Antiquity, met at the Goose and Gridiron tavern near to St. Paul's Cathedral. It was the yearly custom of the lodge to parade from the tavern to a nearby church to celebrate St. John's Day in summer, and Preston maintained that the lodge did not need permission from Grand Lodge for this parade. As the lodge had been one of the founders of Grand Lodge, he asserted that Grand Lodge could not take away a privilege that predated the formation of Grand Lodge itself. Grand Lodge disagreed, and the quarrel escalated. Preston enraged the Grand Lodge so greatly that they expelled Preston from the fraternity!

Preston and his Masonic friends took revenge on Grand Lodge by forming their own grand lodge—the Grand Lodge of England South of the River Trent. And for ten years, until the quarrel was resolved, this rogue group plagued Grand Lodge. When the quarrel was over, Preston was restored to good standing with Grand Lodge, and it is a good thing that he was. He went on to publish a famous book, *Illustrations of Masonry*, in 1772, which is the source of our Masonic lectures to this day. Had the quarrel never been resolved, and Preston remained expelled, it is entirely possible that our lectures today would be significantly different.

The issue behind the quarrel, however, was the concern that unregulated parading by lodges would bring the fraternity into disrepute. There was good reason for this concern. One of the famous pictures of this period was produced by Bro. William Hogarth, a member of a London lodge, and a well-known engraver. One of his engravings shows the master of a Masonic lodge, wearing his apron and jewel, going home late at night through the streets of London, accompanied by his tiler. He is obviously roaring drunk, and is singing at the top of his lungs as he staggers down the street. Hogarth adds a bit of humor to this otherwise pathetic example of Masonic "publicity" by showing a lady at an upper window throwing the contents of a chamber pot out the window and down onto the hapless master and his tiler.

To this day there are some remnants of this era in Freemasonry. First, permission of Grand Lodge is still required for Masons to wear their regalia in public—usually granted now through the district inspector. Secondly, all Masons are anxious when some Masons forget that they are custodians of the public image of Freemasonry, and do things that reflect negatively upon our organization. It is well to remember that every time we walk out the door we will be someone's idea of what a Mason is that day. We are proud to let others know that we are Freemasons, and that pride carries with it a responsibility to exemplify the best of the teachings of Freemasonry when we are not in lodge.

The parades of Freemasonry in the eighteenth century were a form of "theater" for the Masons of that era. They enjoyed letting others know about their membership by parading in public. But they also attracted a lot of negative attention – some of it deserved—and for this reason we developed regulations to control our public appearances. These regulations are still in place after almost three centuries. But there is also the "theater" of how we behave in public as individual Masons. Our ceremonies are of interest to the public today, as they were in London long ago. And our individual behavior as Masons is also of interest to the public today as it was then. Just remember that today you will be someone's idea of a Mason. What you do will make a positive difference for our image.

CONCERNING GOD AND RELIGION

By John L. Cooper III
California Freemason, August – September 2012

The question of the connection between Freemasonry and religion is not an easy topic to tackle. On the one hand, Freemasons are adamant that Freemasonry is not a religion, and not a substitute for religion. It encourages its members to be active in the faith community to which they belong, but does not favor or promote any particular faith. On the other hand, Freemasonry requires that all its members have a belief in God. It begins and ends its meetings with prayer. Members take their promises as Masons on a book sacred to their religion, and (at least in the United States) a Bible is always prominently displayed in the center of the room whenever a lodge is in session. Its rituals have frequent references to God, and to the meaning that a belief in God has for an individual Mason. Why is this?

It would be easy just to say that requiring a belief in God is a part of our heritage, and a part of the fabric of Freemasonry. It is, but it is also something more. In order to understand why, we must return to the formative period of modern Freemasonry (what Masons call "speculative Freemasonry") in the seventeenth and eighteenth centuries in Great Britain. All contemporary Freemasonry comes from lodges in the British Isles, and from the first grand lodges which were formed there beginning in 1717 with the grand lodge in London. In those days a belief in God and in a revealed religion was universal. No one questioned whether God existed, nor that a man should be a member of the religion which God had revealed to mankind. The problem was, which religion? Europe had been torn apart by religious wars starting with the Reformation when Martin Luther nailed his 95 theses to a church door in Wittenberg in 1517. Although the wars started as a conflict between Protestants and Catholics, over the next 200 years it became a conflict between Protestant churches as well. In fact, religion had become the source of murderous conflicts which tore society apart. It was into this situation that Freemasonry emerged.

Freemasonry was a brotherhood, and as such believed that its members should support one another and trust one another as brothers would do in a natural family. But how could this be the case if religious conflicts prevented it? How could a Mason from one religion consider himself to be a brother with a Mason from a competing religion when those religions were at war with one another? The answer was worked out in the early years Freemasonry, and this is the story.

Just six years after the formation of the first grand lodge in 1717, the young Masonic organization adopted one of the foundational documents of our worldwide fraternity. Grand Lodge had asked one of its prominent members, a Presbyterian minister by the name of James Anderson, to write a set of rules to govern the new society, and as a part of the project, he submitted a list of six "charges" to his grand lodge. Based on a free interpretation of the "Old Charges" of the manuscript constitutions, portions of which had traditionally been read at the "making of a mason," Anderson may have envisioned that a similar practice would emerge using these six "modernized" statements about Freemasonry. Regardless of the intent, the Six Charges became the standard interpretation of the craft for a generation, and still remain an important source for understanding the fundamental principles of our institution.

The First Charge, with the title of "Concerning God and Religion," was probably the most important. It set forth clearly the position of Freemasonry concerning the relationship of an individual Mason and his loyalty to God as understood within his own religious community. It answered the fundamental question of how a man could be a brother to someone who did not share his religion without diminishing the loyalty he owed to that religion, and to God as he understood Him. The First Charge of 1723 has become the foundation of Freemasonry's position on the issue of religion to this day.

Freemasonry's answer to the bigotry and hatred of the partisans of competing religions was to search for that which the warring parties had in common rather than that which divided them. It assumed that beneath every particular expression of religious opinion was a common thread of goodness and truth which, if properly understood, could draw men together rather than push them apart. Anderson was too astute a student of history to believe that religious differences could be disregarded, or replaced by some sort of an amalgam of all religions. He was instead interested in how men (and women for that matter) could learn to respect the strongly held beliefs of others without engaging in the destructive behavior that caused such murderous activity by human beings toward one another. Freemasonry held the answer for him: learn to respect and appreciate the religious beliefs that others hold so dear by looking for the good and the true in others. It was this belief that was to transform Freemasonry into the power for good that it has exercised ever since.

Anderson, and Grand Lodge itself, knew that focusing on what is good and what is true in the lives of others puts us on a different footing. Instead of talking about what divides us, it causes us to talk about what unites us. Freemasonry thus becomes a "center of union," to use Anderson's apt phrase, a place where we can become "friends and brothers" without fear of compromising our own convictions.

Sectarian religion and partisan politics are not discussed in a Masonic lodge, or in a Masonic setting. That does not mean that neither is important to a Mason. Far from it. Masons can be deeply religious as well as deeply passionate about political beliefs, and often are. But all Masons share a respect for the beliefs of others that binds them together in a brotherhood which can only occur if they share a commitment to finding that which is good and true in others. This affirmation is at the heart of our respect for one another, and the foundation of that brotherly love and affection which is the envy of the world.

ONE LODGE OR FIFTY?
George Washington and the "American Doctrine"

By John L. Cooper III
California Freemason, October – November 2012

Many Masons know that President George Washington was a Mason, and that he served as the master of Alexandria Lodge No. 22 (now Alexandria-Washington Lodge No. 22) in Alexandria, Virginia, while serving as president of the United States. What many do not know is that there was a movement to make him the grand master of a grand lodge of the United States of America, which would have merged all the individual state grand lodges into one national organization. President Washington turned down this offer, and thus no national grand lodge ever came into existence. It may have been one of the best gifts that our brother, George Washington, gave to American Freemasonry.

Before the American Revolution, lodges in the thirteen colonies owed allegiance to one of three different grand lodges: They held charters from one of two grand lodges in England (either the Moderns or the Ancients), or from the Grand Lodge of Scotland. The Grand Lodge of Ireland also chartered some lodges in connection with military and naval units, and one such lodge was later the source of Prince Hall Freemasonry. When the Treaty of Paris was signed in 1783, recognizing the American colonies as independent states, new grand lodges were quickly organized in each of the former English colonies. These state grand lodges absorbed the lodges within their boundaries, and became the source of legitimate Freemasonry in the United States. But just as each state was jealous of its own prerogatives as a "sovereign unit" in the emerging United States of America, so these thirteen grand lodges jealously guarded their own sovereignty in the world of Freemasonry. It was from this beginning that Freemasonry developed in America, with each new state forming its own grand lodge. Eventually there were fifty one grand lodges in the United States—one for each state, and one for the District of Columbia.

The consequences of this development were enormous, not only for American Freemasonry, but for Freemasonry in general. Before the thirteen state grand lodges were created, it was uncertain how a new grand lodge could be created. That question was settled as far as the United States was concerned, and this had an impact on the rest of the Masonic world. A new grand lodge in the United States was formed when five regular lodges, holding charters from a variety of other state grand lodges, surrendered the charters from their original grand lodges and then bound themselves together in a new grand lodge. This principle prevented arguments as to which grand lodge should control the lodges in the new states as they were added to the Union, and permanently settled the question of the legitimacy of these new grand lodges. The problems which had plagued grand lodges in Europe about the authority of new lodges to govern themselves had been solved. All that was required was that the lodges in an emerging state agree to form a new grand lodge, and that settled that question. The grand lodges which had issued the original charters to form lodges in the new territories and states no longer had any say over the lodges which they had created.

This peculiarly "American Doctrine" of how grand lodges are created is still one of the best models in the world. It leaves the power to form new grand lodges in the hands of the lodges themselves, and recognizes the rights of lodges to choose their new home. This power was exercised by five lodges in California on April 19, 1850, when they met to form the Grand Lodge of California. Each of these lodges held a charter or dispensation from a grand lodge "Back East," but there was never a question as to whether they had the right to surrender their charters to the grand lodge which had created them, and to receive a charter from the newly-formed Grand Lodge of California. In contemporary language, these lodges exercised their privileges in a democracy to become independent, and to form an independent grand lodge which would meet their unique needs in a new environment. Nothing could be more American than this freedom of choice, and it all should be credited to President George Washington. He believed in the uniqueness of Freemasonry as much as he believed in the uniqueness of the United States of America. By turning down the offer to make him "General Grand Master" of the United States America, he guaranteed the harmony that is a salient characteristic of American Freemasonry to this day. The Grand Lodge of Free and Accepted Masons of the State of California is the result of this wise decision on the part of our first president.

In addition to being the Father of His Country, Bro. George Washington is the Father of American Freemasonry.

THE POWER OF THE PEN
Gotthold Lessing and Masonic tolerance

By John L. Cooper III
California Freemason, December – January 2013

The saying "The pen is mightier than the sword" was coined by Edward Bulwer-Lytton in a play he wrote in 1839. But the phrase, had it been invented earlier, might have been the defining characteristic of a Freemason in eighteenth century Germany who changed the course of German Masonic history. His name was Gotthold Lessing, and this is his story.

Born at Kamenz, Germany, on January 22, 1729, Gotthold Ephraim Lessing was almost a contemporary of Bro. George Washington, who was born in 1732. As with our own first president, Freemasonry changed the life of Lessing, and through him, Freemasonry in his own country.

Freemasonry as we know it dates from 1717 when the first grand lodge was formed in London, England. In 1723 the new grand lodge at London adopted a regulation declaring that Freemasonry was to be open to all men regardless of their religious affiliation, with the only requirement being a belief in a Supreme Being. In the 1720s Freemasonry had its first Jewish members, and tolerance toward all religions became a defining landmark in Freemasonry. But as Freemasonry spread to the continent this principle of toleration did not follow with it, and in Germany in the eighteenth century Freemasonry was restricted to members of the Christian religion.

Gotthold Ephraim Lessing enrolled at the University of Leipzig in 1746, and began a journey of personal enlightenment that eventually led him to become a Freemason on October 14, 1770, at Hamburg. It was a logical step for a man whose life by that time had become a passion for learning. The only problem was that his best friend, Moses Mendelssohn, was Jewish and therefore could not become a Mason with him. Out of this personal struggle Lessing created one of the great works of Masonic literature, and caused German Freemasonry to open its doors to men of all faiths.

The work which Lessing wrote is called *Ernst und Falk*, and it is cast in the literary form of a dialogue between two friends. The format is familiar, because Plato used it in writing his dialogues some two thousand years earlier. As with the Socratic dialogues of Plato, Lessing was able to bring the reader into the picture by having him listen in on what purports to be a private conversation.

In Lessing's dialogue, Falk is a new Mason, and he is talking with his friend about Freemasonry. His friend asks him why he became a Mason, and Falk—like many new Masons—doesn't have a very good answer. Ernst asks Falk if he is a Mason, and Falk says, "I think I am." This vague answer sparks a conversation on how a Mason would know that he is a Mason – in other words, is being a Mason something more than just being a member of a Masonic lodge? Today we would probably phrase the question, "Is being a Mason something more than just having a dues card indicating that you have paid your dues to a Masonic lodge?" At the end of the conversation, Falk has a much clearer understanding of what it means to be a Mason – an understanding that is probably expressed best in a play which Lessing later wrote to expand upon the need to truly understand what Freemasonry should mean to a Mason. In his play, *Nathan the Wise*, this description of Freemasonry sums up Lessing's understanding of the impact it should have on every Mason:

> Therefore, let each one imitate this love;
> So, free from prejudice, let each one aim
> To emulate his Brethren in the strife
> To prove the virtues of his several ring,
> By offices of kindness and of love,
> And trust in God. And if, in years to come,
> The virtues of the ring shall reappear
> Amongst your children's children, then, once more
> Come to this judgment-seat. A greater far
> Than I shall sit upon it, and decide.
> So spake the modest judge.

The play was about three brothers whose father gave each one a gold ring—only one of which was the "true" gold ring. The trick was to find out which was the true ring, and the three brothers went before a famous judge to see if he could tell them. He said that the wearer of the true ring would be loved by everyone, while those who wore the false rings would not. You can guess what happened. Each of the brothers lived his life so that he would be the most loved, and as a result the "one true ring" had actually become three "true rings." Freemasonry, according to Lessing, does that. It transforms each of us by causing us to practice kindness and love.

Lessing did not live to see German Freemasonry become open to men of all religious faiths, for he died in 1781. But his influence eventually won out, and by the nineteenth century Freemasons who were Jewish sat down in lodge beside their brethren who were Christian, in a new understanding of the true meaning of brotherhood.

THE EIGHTEENTH CENTURY INTERNET
The first flurries of information exchange took a tangible format

By John L. Cooper III
California Freemason, February – March 2013

Most historians credit the creation of the Internet to the 1960s when government joined with commercial interests to create the first "robust, fault-tolerant, and distributed computer networks" (according to the "Internet" entry in Wikipedia). The main feature of the Internet is its ability to exchange information, and this exchange has created a new ability to share information with an almost limitless audience around the world. While the technology behind the Internet is important, it is what is done with that technology that is far more significant. The Internet has created the ability to instantly share information and receive feedback almost as quickly. The resultant dialogue between those who use the Internet has revolutionized the access to information, and how information is used. But it may come as a surprise that Freemasonry benefited from what might be termed the "Eighteenth Century Internet" long before Freemasons took to cyberspace to talk about the mysteries of Masonry.

The "Eighteenth Century Internet" was not electronic, and it used a technology which was centuries old by the time that organized grand lodge Freemasonry emerged in London in 1717. The printing of books was invented in China, but the invention of moveable type by Johannes Gutenberg around 1439 made printing practical for mass publication of books. At first, book-length publications were the norm, but soon "small books" turned up – booklets concerned with promoting ideas, and which led to the publication of other booklets contradicting those previously published, and leading to the combat of ideas in print. Eventually these smaller publications led to the printing of "pamphlets" – booklets of a temporary nature dealing with current topics that could be sold almost immediately after they were printed. These "pamphlet wars" were a characteristic of the years leading up to the Civil War in England (1642-1651), and for the next century and a half, the "battle of pamphlets" was common on the political and religious fronts. It should therefore come as no surprise that when Freemasonry emerged into modern times that it, too, would become the subject and object of pamphlet wars.

Although the printing of pamphlets and their distribution and sale is not as quick as exchanging information on the Internet today, it was much quicker than had ever been the case in earlier times when books were the primary means of disseminating new information. As Freemasonry became better known to the public in the 1720s, a series of pamphlets were published purporting to reveal the secrets of this mysterious society. In the beginning the fraternity ignored the pamphlets, believing that the less said the better. But soon Freemasons were responding to attacks on the fraternity by publishing their own pamphlets. The Masonic scholars, Douglas Knoop, G.P. Jones, and Douglas Hamer collected and reprinted some of the most important pamphlets from the 1720s in their book, *Early Masonic Pamphlets*. Students today can, therefore, read publications from the pamphlet wars of the early eighteenth century.

Today lots of information about Freemasonry is posted on the Internet—some of it accurate, and some of it very inaccurate. The same thing can be said of the Masonic pamphlets printed in the 1720s in London. Since many of them were published to attack Freemasonry by exposing its ritual, there is no way to know if the rituals so exposed accurately represented Freemasonry of those days. But in 1723 a group of Masons set out to beat the pamphleteers at their own game. The story was told by S. Brent Morris, one of America's foremost Masonic scholars of today, and here is a short version of this fascinating episode in the Masonic pamphlet wars of the 1720s.

For many years Masonic students have known of a pamphlet printed in 1723 called *A Mason's Examination*, and distributed through the Flying Post – a pamphleteering printer in London. It purported to reveal the secrets of the Masons by exposing the "catechism", or "questions and answers" which were the form in which Masonic lectures after the conferral of the degrees were given in those days. In 1998 Bro. Morris was given a copy of a pamphlet which had been published in the *Post-Boy* (note the similarity to the publisher, the Flying Post), and which was a response to the earlier publication the previous April of *A Mason's Examination*. The *Post-Boy* pamphlet purported to be the true exposure of the secrets of the Freemasons, as opposed to what were termed the pretended secrets of *A Mason's Examination*. If the story had ended here, it would have been just another "pamphlet war" between Masons and their detractors, or perhaps between competing enemies of Freemasonry. But then the Masons, who had concocted the exposure in the *Post-Boy,* did something ingenious.

In *The Free-Mason's Accusation and Defence*, a father, purportedly writing to his son, makes an extended reference to the "examination" of the Freemasons published in *The Post Boy*. The relevant statement begins as follows:

> I remember, when I was last in Town, there was a Specimen of their Examinations published in the *Post-Boy*; but so industrious were the Masons to suppress it that in a Week's time not one of the Papers was to be found; where-ever they saw 'em they made away with them.

The excerpt, above, is from Bro. Morris' paper on the subject published in *Heredom*, the annual publication of the Scottish Rite Research Society (Vol. 7, 1998). In order to get the *Post-Boy* version to be considered as the "authentic" publication of the secrets of Freemasonry, they bought up all the copies of the version they had published that they could! And naturally everyone thought that these must be the "real" secrets if the Masons were so anxious to pick up and destroy every copy! However, the *Post-Boy* "exposure" of the ritual was a hoax. The Masons in London had published a bogus ritual, and then bought up as many copies as they could in order to make people think that these were the real secrets! It was a clever scheme, and it seemed to work. By that time no one could trust any of the pamphlets, and the pamphlet wars essentially came to an end.

Pamphlets were the "instant publications" of their day, and just as the Internet today can be the battleground of competing political and religious opinions, so the printing press in the eighteenth century was the technological instrument of similar battles. Freemasonry participated in these battles—both those who opposed it, and those who supported it. And just as today there are hoaxes circulating around the Internet, so hoaxes about Freemasonry circulated from the "instant printing" of pamphlets in the eighteenth century. Freemasons in 1723 used the "Eighteenth Century Internet" to counter the attacks on the fraternity, and used it very cleverly. If they had today's Internet available to them, they might have done even more damage to their detractors. But they did enough, and it is still a fascinating story!

MASONIC CHARITY—A HISTORICAL PERSPECTIVE
The fraternal commitment to relief has defined the institution of Freemasonry

By John L. Cooper III
California Freemason, April – May 2013

Each year the United Grand Lodge of England selects some prominent Mason to be the "Prestonian Lecturer" for the year – fulfilling the wishes of William Preston, the author of our Masonic ritual lectures, who left money in his estate for "some well-informed Mason to deliver annually a Lecture on the First, Second, or Third Degree of the Order of Masonry according to the system practiced in the Lodge of Antiquity during his Mastership." In 1993 the Prestonian Lecturer was Bro. John Hamill, a prominent Masonic scholar, who chose as his topic "Masonic Charity." Bro. Hamill made several important observations in his lecture, and I want to share some of them with you.

Our early brethren understood relief to mean the alleviating of the suffering of a brother, or the dependents of a deceased brother, by giving money or sustenance until circumstances improved. In modern times we see relief in its wider context of charity that is not simply providing money to relieve distress but actually caring and giving of our time and talents in the service of our communities as a whole and not just to our brethren and their dependents.

Bro. Hamill reminds us that one of the earliest tasks undertaken by the new grand lodge in 1717 was the creation of a central "charity fund" for use by the lodges. In 1727, the first charity fund beyond that of an individual lodge was created. A committee was established to dispense charity from this fund and its treasurer was named "grand treasurer" – the first use of this title. The committee received requests for assistance, and could grant up to five guineas without a vote of grand lodge for the relief of a distressed brother, his wife, widow, or orphans. This was a generous gift for those in need.

Economic historians have painted a bleak picture of poverty in eighteenth century England. The bottom twenty percent of the population were deemed the very poor, and their lives were ones of daily misery. Local churches (parishes) were responsible for poor relief, and only the old and disabled were entitled. Children whose parents were too poor to support them were sent to work for free as "apprentices." A law of 1697 required anyone receiving public assistance to wear a blue or red "P" (for "pauper") on their clothes. Those who were able to work, but could not find work, were whipped—for refusing to take non-existent jobs. It is estimated that during the first half of the eighteenth century half the population lived at the subsistence level—barely able to find enough money to stay alive.

It is against this background that the earliest Masonic charity needs to be seen. Masons in the eighteenth century had inherited the practice of helping their most needy members from the operative stonemason days of the Middle Ages. By the time that the Charity Committee had come into existence in 1727 the nature of charity had changed from simply taking care of a brother and his family on a building site to the actual giving of money to help out those in need. And such charity was generous by the standards of the day. Freemasons did not treat their less fortunate brethren as social outcasts. They did not beat a member who could not find work to support his family. They did not sell the children of a member of the lodge to work almost as slave labor for an unscrupulous employer. And they did not require those who were recipients of Masonic charity to wear a letter designating them as "paupers." What Masonic charity did was to treat those less fortunate as friends and brothers—an unheard of idea in the early eighteenth century.

Bro. Hamill points out in his Prestonian Lecture that Masonic charity is so important that it can almost be considered a landmark.

If we define a landmark as being something in Freemasonry, which if it were removed, its removal would materially alter the essence of our Institution, then Charity is certainly a landmark. Without the second of its three Grand Principles, Freemasonry would be a different organization.

The practice of charity may truly be said to be a landmark, for if it were removed from Freemasonry, its removal would materially alter the very nature of our institution. The words of William Preston are still heard by every Entered Apprentice as he begins his journey into Freemasonry:

> To relieve the distressed is a duty incumbent on all men, but particularly on Masons, who are linked together by an indissoluble chain of sincere affection. To soothe the unhappy, to sympathize with their misfortunes, to compassionate their miseries, and to restore peace to their troubled minds, is the great aim we have in view. On this basis we form our friendships and establish our connections.

Sir Christopher Wren and the architectural renaissance in London after the Great Fire

By John L. Cooper III
California Freemason, June – July 2013

Early on a Sunday morning, September 2, 1666, a fire broke out in a bakery on Pudding Lane, in the center of the City of London. By Sunday evening winds had created an inferno which destroyed most of the historic city within the ancient Roman walls, including St. Paul's Cathedral atop Ludgate Hill. Thousands of homes were destroyed, as well as 87 parish churches, and the British capital was reduced to ruins. By the time the fire had burned itself out on the following Wednesday, the great city was no more. Some 100,000 people were left homeless, and the smoldering ruins prevented a quick return to the houses that remained untouched.

St. Paul's Cathedral was the most important symbol of the old city of London, and King Charles II moved immediately to replace the destroyed church to show his commitment to the British capital. The architect, Christopher Wren, had been retained even before the Great Fire to remodel the old cathedral, and it was natural that he would be given the assignment to build its replacement. The building that arose on the site was truly a monument to the man who was undoubtedly the greatest British architect of his day. In the month of June, 1675, the first stone of the new cathedral was laid by the stonemasons of London under the direction of Thomas Strong, one of the two Master Masons that Wren appointed to oversee the construction. There is no evidence that these two Masons belonged to the Masonic lodge which met at the Goose and Gridiron tavern across the square from the cathedral site, but it is possible that they were members. We know that this lodge was a "time immemorial lodge," and one of the four lodges which founded the first grand lodge in 1717. The lodge is still in existence, with the name and number of "The Lodge of Antiquity No. 2" on the rolls of the United Grand Lodge of England.

The new cathedral was built of Portland stone in a late renaissance style, which was Wren's version of English Baroque. The structure is a tribute to his understanding of the beauty and harmony of classical architecture melded with the historic cruciform style of ancient cathedrals. The building was declared complete by Parliament on Christmas Day, 1711. It was Wren's masterpiece— the culmination of his life as an architect— and he is thus considered to be one of the most acclaimed architects in

English history. In addition to St. Paul's Cathedral, he built fifty-two more churches in London after the Great Fire, as well as some secular buildings of note.

In keeping with his time, Wren came to the study of architecture from the study of the liberal arts and sciences, and especially astronomy, mathematics and geometry. He was a founder of the Royal Society, the world's first scientific organization, which at his death in 1723 included many of the most famous names in the world of science and mathematics. He was knighted by the king on November 14, 1673, and thus is known to history as Sir Christopher Wren.

There is no evidence that Wren was a Freemason, although in 1738 the premier grand lodge claimed that he was. In fact the Constitutions of 1738 explicitly stated that his "neglect" of the craft as "grand master" due to his advancing years was responsible for the decision in 1717 to form the world's first grand lodge. We may never know for sure if England's most celebrated architect was a Mason, but the monument that he left in the magnificent cathedral in the heart of London is truly a tribute to the builder's art. He certainly associated with prominent Freemasons such as John Desaguliers, who was grand master in 1719, and who was also secretary to the Royal Society when Wren was a member.

At his death he was buried in the cathedral which was his greatest achievement, and this inscription was carved on his tomb:

SUBTUS CONDITUR HUIUS ECCLESIÆ ET VRBIS CONDITOR CHRISTOPHORUS WREN, QUI VIXIT ANNOS ULTRA NONAGINTA, NON SIBI SED BONO PUBLICO. LECTOR SI MONUMENTUM REQUIRIS CIRCUMSPICE OBIIT XXV FEB ÆTATIS XCI AN MDCCXXIII.

In English it reads:

Here in its foundations lies the architect of this church and city, Christopher Wren, who lived beyond ninety years, not for his own profit but for the public good. Reader, if you seek his monument—look around you. Died 25 Feb. 1723, age 91.

Whether or not Sir Christopher Wren was a Freemason as alleged by the Grand Lodge in 1738, no greater tribute to any Mason could be given than this. The lives that we lead, "not for [our] own profit but for the public good ..." is the best and most lasting monument to our work as Freemasons. At the end of our earthly journey, what we did in life will be a far greater monument than any of marble or brass. It may well be said of each of us when we lay down our working tools, "Reader, if you seek his monument—look around."

SCHOOLS OF VIRTUE

Early American lodges provided unprecedented opportunities for young men to learn values and practice leadership

By John L. Cooper III
California Freemason, August-Septmber 2013

In eighteenth century America, Masonic lodges were schools of leadership for rising middle-class men in the years leading up to the American Revolution. They were places where ambitious young men could meet and mingle with older successful men who could open doors for them as they rose in society. It must be remembered that Colonial American society was an extension of British society in those days, a society still governed by a landed aristocracy of inherited powers and influence. Although America was a more open society than that which prevailed in the British homeland, many of the Colonies were dominated by inherited wealth. This was particularly so in the middle Colonies and in the South, where slavery was also an important institution. Inherited wealth was less important in the New England Colonies, but nevertheless the mercantile class dominated social and political structures, and there was little free access to the governing class even by dint of hard work and individual enterprise. We are so used to a relatively "classless" society in America today that it is difficult to imagine that it once was very different.

George Washington is an example of how Freemasonry helped open doors that would have otherwise shut him out of leadership opportunities in Virginia—one of the most aristocratic of the Thirteen Colonies and a society governed at the time by what were termed the "Tidewater Gentry." The term "Tidewater" referred to the coastal region of the Old Dominion, as it was fondly known, and the aristocratic owners of large estates controlled the government of this royal colony. Although the governor was appointed by the king in distant London, the legislature of the Colonies, the House of Burgesses, had considerable influence and power. When coupled with the Governor's Council—which could veto legislation adopted by the House of Burgesses, the Colony was firmly in the hands of men of wealth and stature.

It is against this background that Masonic lodges in the Colonies introduced a new element. Lodges attracted men of wealth and influence in the Colonies, but they also attracted rising young men whose business acumen impressed the older leadership. On November 4, 1752, a 20-year-old George Washington was initiated an Entered Apprentice Mason in Fredericksburg Lodge No. 4 near Mt. Vernon. Steven Bullock, in his book *Revolutionary Brotherhood: Freemasonry and the Transformation of the American Social Order, 1730-1840*, makes it clear that Freemasonry was one of the most important vehicles in Colonial and post-Colonial America for upward mobility. Freemasonry promoted the idea of equality and advancement based on merit—and these two virtues were essential to the rising leadership class in America.

But was Freemasonry just another "networking" organization for young and aspiring businessmen? Bullock doesn't think so. The major difference between Masonic lodges in that era and a number of similar organizations where men networked (to use a contemporary term) is that these lodges perceived themselves as schools of virtue. In other words, they were places where values were taught along with opportunities to practice leadership. And it was Freemasonry that helped transfer these virtues to the public sphere for the emerging government in the states and eventually at the national level. According to Bullock:

> The people's character ultimately determined the health and prosperity of a society without the strong government and traditional restraints that had previously undergirded the social order ... George Washington's 1796 Farewell Address thus called morality one of the 'great Pillars of human happiness' and 'political prosperity.' Masonry helped to provide the foundation for this building, training and teaching Americans to reinforce 'the duties of men and Citizens.' As Washington noted to his brothers only a few months later, America needed to become what Masonry already was: 'a lodge for the virtues.'

Leadership, whether in private life or in public life, must be based on principles if it is to truly be of any value. Freemasons understood that, and thus introduced the concept of principled leadership to the world. It was more than just a place to network with others who were upwardly mobile in Colonial times, and it is more—much more—today. Today, a candidate for the degrees of Masonry is asked a very important question at the start of his journey:

> Do you seriously declare, upon your honor, that unbiased by friends and uninfluenced by mercenary motives, you freely and voluntarily offer yourself as a candidate for the mysteries of Masonry?

160

It is likely that Bro. George Washington was asked a similar question at the beginning of his Masonic journey. Mercenary motives are not a part of Freemasonry, for although Masonic lodges are schools of leadership, they are also schools of virtue.

OUR ANCIENT FRIEND AND BROTHER
The teachings of Pythagoras continue to inspire our fraternity

By John L. Cooper III
California Freemason, October – November 2013

Mathematics, the "queen of the sciences," has always had a preeminent place in the liberal arts, and in Masonry. It appears twice in the list, as both arithmetic and geometry, and we are told in our ritual that geometry is "the first and noblest of sciences, and the basis upon which the superstructure of Freemasonry is erected."

This idea is a very old one in Freemasonry, for the *Old Charges*, also called the *Gothic Constitutions*, place geometry in a premier position amongst the liberal arts and sciences. The *Regius Manuscript*, c. 1390, says (in modern English translation):

In that time, through good geometry,
This honest craft of good masonry
Was ordained and made in this manner ....

Many of these constitutions refer to Euclid as having carried the knowledge of Masonry to other lands, and the references are generally to geometry. Euclid (c. 325-265 BC) was called the "father of geometry," and Euclid's *Elements* remains a primary geometry textbook today. In the 47th Proposition of his *Elements*, Euclid provided a proof of the relationship of the sides of a right-angle triangle so that when the proportions are correct, a right-angle is formed. The importance to stonemasons of this geometric principle is evident, because in order to construct stone buildings properly, a square corner must first be established. The use of geometry in general, and the 47th Proposition in particular, was therefore an essential element in operative masonry, and this importance was transferred to speculative Freemasonry in a symbolic sense.

The 47th Proposition of Euclid is more familiarly known as the "Pythagorean theorem," for its discovery was attributed in ancient times to the Greek philosopher, Pythagoras. We know very little about Pythagoras as a person, and almost as little about his teachings. He is supposed to have been born on the island of Samos around 570 BC, to have established a school at Crotona, in Italy, and to have died around 495 BC.

Kitty Ferguson, in her book, *The Music of Pythagoras: How an Ancient Brotherhood Cracked the Code of the Universe and Lit the Path from Antiquity to Outer Space,"* noted that:

Pythagoras and the devotees who surrounded him during his lifetime were obsessively secretive ... The earliest written evidence about Pythagoras himself that modern scholarship accepts as genuine consists of six short fragments of text from the century after his death, found not in their originals but in works of ancient authors who either saw the originals or were quoting from earlier secondary copies.

Despite the conclusions of modern scholars about the difficulty of knowing much about Pythagoras, he has a firm place in Masonic lore and ritual. In 1772, William Preston, a past master of the Lodge of Antiquity No. 1 in London, published the *Illustrations of Masonry*—a collection of material then in use as lectures in Masonic lodges in England and Scotland. This book was used by Thomas Smith Webb, an American Mason, in 1797, to create his famous *Freemasons Monitor*, which was drawn upon by American grand lodges as the source of the lectures of the three degrees of ancient craft Masonry. Preston is thus the "grandfather" of our lectures as used today, and we find in Preston words and phrases which are very familiar. In *Illustrations of Masonry*, he writes:

Masonry ... is not only the most ancient, but the most moral Institution that ever subsisted; as every character, figure, and emblem, depicted in the lodge, has a moral meaning, and tends to inculcate the practice of virtue on those who behold it.

This material is not included in our present lectures, but we still reference Pythagoras as our "ancient friend and brother" in the long form of the lecture of the third degree.

In the eighteenth century, Masons were fascinated by the philosophy of Pythagoras, and by the "secret brotherhood" which they believed him to have established at Crotona. The link between his famous Pythagorean theorem, made this even more important. Kitty Ferguson goes on to say:

Those six early fragments are not, however, the full extent of the available evidence about the Pythagoreans.... Philolaus, a not-so-secretive Pythagorean, wrote a book ... revealing that early Pythagoreans proposed that the Earth moves and is not the center of the cosmos. Plato... tried to incorporate what he thought of as a Pythagorean curriculum – the "quadrivium" – at his Academy in Athens. Aristotle and his pupils wrote extensively about the Pythagoreans a few years later... It seems no other group has ever made such an effort to remain secret, or succeeded so well, as the Pythagoreans did – and yet become so celebrated and influential over such an astonishingly long period of time.

The teachings of Pythagoras are thus a part of Freemasonry, and while Freemasonry is not a secret society in the same sense that the school of Pythagoras was, like Pythagoras himself, and his school, we too have become "celebrated and influential over an astonishingly long period of time."

THE ART OF MEMORY

By John L. Cooper III
California Freemason, December - January 2014

As Freemasonry in the United States began to attract fewer and fewer members after 1970, Masons looked around for the causes of this decline. As the decline accelerated during the last three decades of the last century, grand lodges began to adopt programs to address this decline, and to change existing requirements for progressing through the degrees of Masonry.

The debate centered around whether it was necessary any longer for candidates to memorize the old candidate proficiencies, and whether it was really necessary to confer the three degrees of ancient craft Masonry only after a candidate had memorized and delivered in open lodge what were often perceived as impediments for Entered Apprentices and Fellow Crafts to become Master Masons. Students of Freemasonry were well aware that these proficiencies had at one time been the lectures delivered to candidates after the conferral of a degree, and only at a later date had candidates been required to memorize them and deliver them in lodge as a condition for advancement to the next degree. If so, then why not abandon this requirement so that it would be easier to become a Master Mason? This, in turn, might encourage men to apply for the degrees of Masonry, and thus stop the decline in membership.

California took this route in 1997, when the delegates to the annual communication removed the requirement that a candidate recite the historic proficiencies, and replaced them with the requirement that the Entered Apprentice and Fellow Craft Masons only needed to memorize the obligation of the degree concerned, along with the words, signs, and modes of recognition, and deliver those in a tiled lodge before he could take the next degree. The proficiency for the Master Mason degree was not similarly shortened, but as the candidate did not need it for advancement beyond that degree, there was no impact on the candidate caused by its retention.

Upon passage of this legislation, Grand Master Anthony P. Wordlow was asked to decide whether the older "long form" proficiencies could still be used. He ruled that they could be used, but the option to do so rested with the candidate alone. At a later time, these shortened proficiencies were augmented with a requirement that the candidate pass a basic education written test pertaining to the degree concerned. But no memory work was associated with the latter requirement as the test was to be an open book examination.

This change has remained somewhat controversial amongst Masons in California, and while honoring the condition in our law that the choice of a "short form" or "long form" proficiency is strictly up to the candidate, candidates are often encouraged to memorize and deliver the long form.

Memorizing the long form of the proficiencies not only has a historic place in Freemasonry, but is actually tied up with our symbolism and ethos. One of the streams of which Freemasonry is composed is the Renaissance Hermetic Tradition. This tradition built upon and expanded the concept of the art of memory, which was thought to be an important skill. In her book, *The Art of Memory*, scholar Frances Yates writes:

> The art of memory is like an inner writing. Those who know the letters of the alphabet can write down what is dictated to them and read out what they have written. Likewise those who have learned mnemonics can set in places what they have heard and deliver it from memory. 'For the places are very much like wax tablets or papyrus, the images like the letters, the arrangement and disposition of the images like the script, and the delivery is like the reading.'

Yates is quoting from a first century BC work called *Ad Herennium*, which caught the interest of philosophers during the Renaissance. It was the concept of this "inner writing" that intrigued them, and which passed into Freemasonry from these philosophers. It is thus that the "art of memory" is an important part of Freemasonry—not just something which must be endured, or even abandoned. And although Masons may differ on how much "memory work" should be required of candidates as they advance, there is little question that memorization performs a much more important function in Freemasonry than just learning some antique language by rote. It is actually a form of inner writing, which gives the candidate an additional dimension of the initiatic process. Our ritual states:

> Tools and implements of architecture most expressive are selected by the Fraternity to imprint upon the memory wise and serious truths; and thus, through the succession of ages, are transmitted unimpaired the most excellent tenets of our Institution.

Although not as commonly known as our other "tools and implements," the art of memory is one of the most important.

A CANDID DISQUISITION
Wellins Calcott and the Masonic culture of fellowship

By John L. Cooper III
California Freemason, February – March 2014

With the creation of the first grand lodge in London in 1717, Freemasonry's popularity boomed. Lodges sought charters from this new Masonic body, and the public's attention to these lodges grew apace. It may have been the secrecy which intrigued them, or the Masonic parades that became somewhat common during the early years after the founding of the grand lodge. But whatever it was, the public wanted to know more about this curious organization, and it was not long before Masons answered that curiosity with publications about Freemasonry intended for the general public. It is from these publications that we catch a glimpse of the culture of early grand lodge Freemasonry, and one of the most important was a book published in 1769 by Bro. Wellins Calcott.

We do not know his original lodge, but in 1758 Calcott was present at a meeting of Lodge No. 71 in Birmingham. Lodge No. 71 was an Ancient's lodge, and not long afterward Calcott joined two Scottish lodges. He was the master of the Lodge of Regularity in London in 1768, and in 1779 he was made an honorary member of Apollo Lodge in York, England. These associations indicate that Calcott was more than casually involved in Freemasonry, and thus it is not surprising that in 1769 he published a book explaining Freemasonry, not only to the members of the craft, but to the public at large.

The title is a rather ponderous one, but not unusual in eighteenth century England: *A Candid Disquisition of the Principles and Practices of the Most Ancient and Honorable Society of Free and Accepted Masons; together with Some Strictures on the Origin, Nature, and Design of that Institution.* It is the earliest of three very influential books on Freemasonry published around the same time. Bro. William Preston published his *Illustrations of Masonry* in 1772, and William Hutchinson published his *The Spirit of Masonry* in 1774. All three books try to answer the question, "What is Freemasonry?" In answering this question, each author describes the culture of Freemasonry as it existed at the beginning of the modern era.

For Wellins Calcott, the purpose of Freemasonry is primarily social in nature. While the teachings and symbolism of Freemasonry are important to him, he is especially interested in how it brings men together in a fellowship of brothers. It is this aspect of Freemasonry which he finds

169

particularly appealing, and he explains that it is from the principle of friendship and fellowship in the lodge that Freemasons have discovered the universality of the human spirit, without regard to language or country. Calcott wrote:

> This principle [of brotherhood] is the bond of peace, and the cement of masonic affection. Free Masons esteem it as a virtue of the most diffusive nature, not to be confined to particular persons, but extended to the whole human race, to administer assistance to whom, is their highest pride and the utmost wish, establishing friendships and forming connections, not by receiving, but conferring benefits.

We find an echo of Calcott in the lecture of the Entered Apprentice degree:

> By the exercise of Brotherly Love we are taught to regard the whole human species as one family, the high and the low, the rich and the poor, who, as created by one Almighty Parent, and inhabitants of the same planet, are to aid, support and protect each other. On this principle Masonry unites men of every country, sect and opinion; and causes true friendship to exist among those who might otherwise have remained at a perpetual distance.

During the eighteenth century, Freemasonry was spreading around the world, and it was this idea of a universal fellowship which enabled it to spread so widely and so rapidly. Calcott points out that this principle is essential to a true understanding of Freemasonry. Freemasonry is not to be confined to particular persons—those who are our immediate acquaintances—"but extended to the whole human race, to administer assistance to whom, is their highest pride and the utmost wish, establishing friendships and forming connections, not by receiving, but conferring benefits."

Friendship and fellowship are thus defining characteristics of a Mason, no less than his commitment to virtue and morality. In a very important sense, fellowship is the culture of Freemasonry. And as it was thus at the beginning of modern Freemasonry, so it is today. We are, indeed, a universal band of brothers, causing "true friendship to exist among those who might otherwise have remained at a perpetual distance."

AT A PERPETUAL DISTANCE

By John L. Cooper III
California Freemason, April - May 2014

In the first degree of Masonry we learn that our fraternity is found "in every country and every clime." This is a sweeping generalization – as it applies only to nations and societies where Freemasonry is allowed to exist – but since Freemasonry is allowed in the vast majority of the world's nations, it is almost true.

Still, the dispersion of Masons throughout the world does not explain how or why Freemasonry is divided into various "orders" or "families," or why these groups may share a common understanding of the nature of Freemasonry within each family, but not across the boundaries that divide one from another. Freemasons from one family may freely mingle with Freemasons of the same family in other parts of the world, but cannot meet together as Freemasons with those of a different family who live across the street. How did this come about?

From the beginning of modern Freemasonry, sometimes called "grand lodge" Freemasonry, the issue of who was entitled to be considered a Freemason was a concern. The first grand lodge, formed in London in 1717, resolved this problem by issuing charters to lodges under its control, and then extending fraternal recognition only to grand lodges in other countries that seemed to share their same basic values and essential organizational principles. These basic values and organizational principles were termed "landmarks," and while there were different ideas as to what truly belonged on a list of landmarks, there were some common principles. One of the most important was that a grand lodge would not be recognized unless it required of all its members a belief in a Supreme Being. Another was the grand lodges would only be recognized if they limited membership to men. There were other requirements as well, but these two were crucial.

However, as Freemasonry evolved, not everyone agreed that these two principles were essential to "authentic" Freemasonry. There was even some ambiguity about the first condition—a belief in a Supreme Being—in the first constitution adopted by the premier grand lodge in London in 1723. It was out of this ambiguity, as well as over concerns about whether women could be Freemasons, that other families of Freemasonry began to emerge. Today the oldest and largest of these families is generally referred to a "regular" Freemasonry, e.g., Freemasonry that adheres to the essential rules as reflected in the landmarks. But another large family

171

has decided that freedom of thought on the subject of belief in a Supreme Being is not incompatible with the fundamentals of Freemasonry, and does not demand this as a condition of membership. This family is known as "progressive" Freemasonry, and usually referred to as "irregular" by the more traditional ("regular") Freemasons. Another, but smaller family consists of lodges and grand lodges which welcome both men and women as members, while still another family welcomes only women.

These separated families of Freemasons all consider themselves to be Freemasons, but they are not so free to acknowledge other families as Freemasons. They all share a common heritage of tradition from the earliest days of Freemasonry, and their lodges and rituals often resemble one another in striking detail. But there is a serious and lasting gulf between these families due to an inability to reconcile what each one considers to be the fundamental organizational principles of Freemasonry.

Is some sense, this situation impairs the purported universality of Freemasonry. However, there are places where these families cooperate across the boundary lines that separate them. They often share scholarly and academic resources that do not involve "recognizing" one another as Freemasons in a strict sense. They also often share cultural activities, such as museum exhibitions. They are increasingly engaged in a dialogue across the boundaries, exploring what they have in common without compromising what each considers to be essential to the definition of a Freemason. There is thus a growing respect for one another between and among these families, without having to resolve the essential differences that divide them. Many of us consider this development encouraging. After all, the hope that Freemasonry would become a "center of union" for those otherwise estranged was clearly stated in the first constitution of the first grand lodge in 1723:

> ... whereby Masonry becomes the Center of Union, and the Means of conciliating true Friendship among Persons that must have remain'd at a perpetual Distance.

MY BROTHER'S KEEPER

By John L. Cooper III
California Freemason, June – July 2014

One of the oldest questions in the world is "Am I my brother's keeper"? The Bible's Book of Genesis brings this question to our attention in the old story of Cain and Abel, handed down to us from the earliest of times. If you remember the story, these two sons of Adam and Eve got into a quarrel after God had apparently accepted the sacrifice of one of the brothers but not the other. The quarrel resulted in the murder of Abel by Cain, and when God asked Cain what happened to his brother, Cain replied with the snide comment, "Am I my brother's keeper?"

His retort to God has thus been handed down to us from antiquity, yet it has never been completely answered: How far am I to go in taking care of my brother? Are there any limits to my responsibilities to him? And if so, what are they?

This is an important question in Freemasonry today. Our Masonic tradition as well as our Masonic law make it clear that each Mason has an obligation to care for his brother Mason, an obligation that also extends to a Mason's family. But what does this obligation entail?

The answer to this question might just be found in the *Old Tiler Talks* by Carl H. Claudy, written in 1925. Listen to this dialogue between a young Mason and the old tiler of his lodge:

> "I am inclined to think that Masons do too much for each other," announced the New Brother.

> "Who has been doing too much for you?" asked the Old Tiler.

> "Why, no one, that I know of."

> "Well, who have you been doing too much for?"

> "Well, er – I wouldn't say I had been doing too much. But we all do too much. It gets to be a burden sometimes."

> "What do you mean, burden?" countered the Old Tiler.

> "A burden is something heavy which you carry, isn't it?" asked the New Brother.

173

"You think what we do for our brethren is a burden?"

"Sometimes it seems that way. Too many calls on our time. Too many calls on our sympathy. Too many calls on our charity. Yes, I think it's a burden."

"Last week I walked to work," answered the Old Tiler. "I don't usually because my rheumatism says walking is too hard a job. My legs," his eyes twinkled, "are a burden to me! But that day it was so bright that the old legs forgot to growl, so I walked. I saw a little lad of about ten looking after a small child of about two, who toppled on his nose and yelled. The ten year old picked up the squalling baby and soothed him, then put him across his shoulder and staggered up the sidewalk with him. I asked him, 'Sonny, isn't that child too heavy for you?' 'Heavy?' he answered me, 'Heavy? Why, sir, he's my brother.'"

"Little brother would have been too heavy for me – maybe because of my old legs and perhaps because he wasn't my brother! The facts are that one weighed 60 pounds and the other 30 pounds. The stagger and the straining arms were facts. The cheeks flushed with effort was a fact. But two years old was brother to ten, and that made him 'not too heavy.'"

"A burden is, after all, what we think it. You would look desperately at the task of carrying a 200-pound sack on your back. But if it were 200 pounds of gold, and it was to be yours after a mile, you wouldn't find it 'too heavy.'"

"Masonry, my son, is a state of mind. You can't put it on the scales or measure it with a scoop. Because it has no material existence it cannot carry a child of two, or a sack of flour. Its burdens are burdens of the heart."

And that just might be Freemasonry's answer to one of the world's oldest questions—"Am I my brother's keeper?"

WHEN THE MASONIC LODGE WAS A UNIVERSITY
Lodge rooms reflect our Masonic quest for knowledge

By John L. Cooper III
California Freemason, August - September 2014

Have you ever wondered why there are two globes atop the pillars near the door to the preparation room in a Masonic lodge? On one pillar is a globe of the earth and on the other is a celestial globe, showing the constellations of the night sky. Masons sometimes refer to them as terrestrial globes. Why are they there? Why would Masons put globes on top of these two pillars, which imitate those that stood before the door of King Solomon's Temple?

When Freemasonry emerged into the modern world in the form that we know it today, there was a thirst for knowledge. Most men had to be self-taught because only the wealthy could afford what we would today call a college education. The ancient traditions and symbols of Freemasonry that lodges had inherited were used to teach their members lessons of morality and ethics.

But enterprising Masons soon saw that they could do much more than that. The symbolism of King Solomon's Temple offered them a splendid opportunity to take Masonic symbolism in a new direction, and to offer members a digest of contemporary education in the arts and sciences, as then understood. In doing so, they modified the original symbols and equipment in a Masonic lodge forever, an example of which is the globes atop the pillars at the entrance of the preparation room.

King Solomon's Temple had long been a source of Masonic legend and symbolism, and stories about it were featured in the old manuscript constitutions, copies of which were considered essential to the true functioning of a Masonic lodge. These manuscript constitutions contained stories that early Masons believed were handed down from antiquity. The pillars before King Solomon's Temple were said to be related to other pillars built by Masons. One of their functions was to preserve the secrets of Masonry, should they be endangered by fire or flood. So, the use of imitation pillars was a natural feature to incorporate into the symbolism of Masonic lodges. Today, these pillars are one of the signature items with which a Masonic lodge is furnished.

The original pillars in front of King Solomon's Temple are described as being topped with lotus blossoms. A lotus blossom is bowl-shaped, so the tops of the pillars had what might be described as pommels or globes, being spherical in design. At some point in the early eighteenth century, an enterprising lodge decided that these pommels could serve a more useful purpose, and they were replaced by the terrestrial and celestial globes that we see today. But why do that? Why take the original symbols of King Solomon's Temple and combine it with a contemporary symbol, such as a terrestrial and celestial globe?

Masonic scholars are still looking for a definitive answer to this question, but I would like to suggest one for your consideration: I believe that they were intended to be symbols of the progressive nature of knowledge. The Fellow Craft degree in Masonry is about knowledge— knowledge of the arts and sciences, and ultimately knowledge of the Great Architect of the Universe, and the relation of this knowledge to our daily life. The charge given to the candidate at the end of the Fellow Craft degree describes Freemasonry as a progressive moral science:

> Masonry is a progressive moral science divided into different degrees; and, as its principles and mystic ceremonies are regularly developed and illustrated, it is intended and hoped that they will make a deep and lasting impression upon your mind.

The people of the time of King Solomon's Temple still believed the world was flat, and would not have understood either the terrestrial or the celestial globes, but the Masonic symbolism to the new Fellow Craft is clear. He is progressing from an "old" understanding of reality to a "new" understanding. The "old" is represented by the ancient pillars and the "new" by the globes. In the rest of the degree, he will be introduced to the function of knowledge itself, represented by the winding staircase. Taken together, the meaning is that in order to progress in Masonry, he must accept that he will leave behind old understanding and embark on a journey into new and fresh understandings. Freemasonry will become his "university of knowledge," not because it has all the answers for him, but because it has all the questions for him. The questing mind is a salient characteristic of a Freemason. And the globes atop the ancient pillars from King Solomon's Temple are a symbol of that quest.

It is in this way that a Masonic lodge is thought of as a "university." Properly understood, a university does not provide a completed education. Its true function is to open the doors to knowledge so that a lifelong commitment to learning results. In a similar way, the Fellow Craft degree is intended to open doors of learning about Masonry. The degree is not intended to teach everything that there is to know about Freemasonry. It is, instead, to create in the Mason a thirst for knowledge, and to teach him that he should have a lifelong commitment to learning – and not just about Freemasonry. In this way, Freemasonry itself becomes the "university of life" for every Mason.